'This astonishing book shares the simple yet largely forgotten secrets to living a happy life … it's a dynamic text book of unfolding consciousness written by someone who has risked all to open his heart … it's a map to love and the manual we have all been waiting for' Susie Anthony, award-winning personal development author/mentor

'This is the best emotional intelligence system I have ever come across. It really works for different types of people' Dr. Bal Rana PhD, psychologist and senior psychology lecturer

'This is an astonishingly powerful tool. I have seen patients with long-term issues, who had previously explored traditional therapies without much success, be totally transformed by FreeMind.' Dr David Morris, General Practitioner and acupuncturist

'Prior to working with Tom, the world was often a cynical, brutal, shallow place. Afterwards, it feels like the sun has come out in my life.' I can feel the warmth on my back, I stand tall and walk forward with confidence. If, like me, you are lucky enough to get the opportunity to work with Tom, you'll never look back.' Chris Randall, business coach

'Tom is truly an extraordinary magician of the mind, deftly weaving images, music and words into a profound experience that transformed my most stubborn of behaviours into new, fresh, healthy ways of seeing and being. Thank you from the bottom of my now much more healthy heart!' Tiu De Haan, celebrant and co-author of the Ripe and Ready book series

'FreeMind is just, well, there are not the words………………. Imagine all the colours in the world, as bright as any could be, a big random set of smiles, the sound of good-humoured belly laughter, some doves flying, the awesome smell of nature, a huge circle of smiling, laughing friends, a loving glance between two people that could write a book, some amazing food, the birds singing at dawn, the sun rising and then setting all at once, spring springing, waves lapping, sunshine we all love, the knowing hoot of an age old owl, the freedom call of power of a male deer in autumn, some happy wagging tails, lolling tongues (dogs not people), children laughing, the soundless sound of snow flakes falling, people singing, drums drumming, stars shooting, water tumbling from a waterfall, and a guitar sweetly echoing the emotion of it all. Well that's Tom's work. I thank him from every cell in my body. And I am sure one day, so will the universe.' Denise McLeod, animal behaviour specialist

'Tom's unique, and I would say ground-breaking, approach to success psychology didn't just teach me a great deal about myself, but also opened my eyes to a whole new way to thinking about human behaviour in general … He provides a straightforward, logical and very practical way of approaching self-development, without any of the wishy-washy psychobabble.' John Hillman, online marketing consultant

THE FREEMIND EXPERIENCE

THE THREE PILLARS OF ABSOLUTE HAPPINESS

TOM FORTES MAYER

WATKINS

Sharing Wisdom Since
1893

This edition published in the USA and Canada 2015 by

Watkins, an imprint of Watkins Media Limited

19 Cecil Court

London WC2N 4HE

enquiries@watkinspublishing.co.uk

Design and typography copyright © Watkins Media Limited, 2015

Text copyright © Tom Fortes Mayer, 2015

1 3 5 7 9 10 8 6 4 2

Designed and typeset by Georgina Hewitt

Printed and bound in Europe

A CIP record for this book is available from the British Library

ISBN: 978-1-78028-801-7

www.watkinspublishing.com

Contents

ACKNOWLEDGMENTS

As I sit here considering who I would like to thank, I am marveling at all the different people who have played a part in bringing this book to fruition. Writing this book has been a rite of passage in itself and I've been shepherded along the way with such love and support.

First, I would like to thank my mother and father for everything they have done for me over the years. I am astounded at the love they have shown me and the support they have given me. I want to thank my sister Deborah for being such an inspiration, and my brother Paul for always believing in me as a writer and encouraging me to tell my story. Thanks also to Gail, Ben and Rachael Fortes Mayer for the love and laughter we always share.

I am deeply grateful for my daughter Portia. Her wild and wonderful spirit is a source of absolute joy in my life that continuously puts everything into perspective. I also want to thank Hester Fortes Mayer for the love, friendship, and commitment she has shown me on our conscious co-parenting journey.

I want to honor Mike Trim, Sarah Jarvis, and their glorious children for showing me the deepest unconditional love during the hardest time of my life. Your love made everything possible again. And a special thanks to Mike for the extraordinary musical scores he has painstakingly created for the FreeMind recordings. Every note is perfect.

I also want to thank Val and Kim Mould for their generosity, belief, and investment in the FreeMind vision; and Denise McLeod for her endless support and encouragement. Thanks also to Maneesh Garg for bringing this work to Nigeria and for teaching me that entrepreneurship is a marathon not a sprint. Thanks also to Nick Seneca Jankel for the endless debates, which have sharpened my understanding of everything I believe in.

I am truly grateful to those friends whom I entrusted with my first, and rather large, manuscript of *The FreeMind Experience*. Helen Royle, David Morris, Chris Randall, Leo Lourie, and Liz Rigby: your feedback made all of the difference. Huge respect must also go to my dear friend Jont who is the world's best-kept musical secret and living saint of not giving up. Thanks also to Brendon Rowen and Helly Perks for the love, laughter, friendship, and general cheerleading.

I must also thank Tania O'Donnell for spotting me, inviting me to submit, and then championing this book all the way through to contract and beyond. That was a blessed and magical beginning to this book. Thanks also to Kelly Thompson and Sandy Draper for the brilliance, care, and attention that you both brought to the editing of this book. I am blown away by your dedication. Thanks also to the countless other people at Watkins who played a part in bringing this book to light.

Thanks to Bill Haynes and Patrick Boucard from Verridian for their passion and vision in bringing FreeMind principles and practices to big business.

Thanks must also go to all the different teachers, mentors, and writers who have made a huge difference in my life. Notably Nisargadatta Maharaj, Ramana Maharshi, AH Almaas, Osho, Marianne Williamson, Tony Robbins, Jon Hansen, Roger Linden, Jan Day and Leora Lightwoman.

Special thanks must also go to Rajyo, Britta, Debbie, and Gina from Celebration of Being. Their beautiful work brought an essential balance to my life and my work that is with me every single day.

I am astounded at all the people that are a part of this book. All of the experiences, upsets, challenges, blessings, and chance encounters along the way that led me to new places, new people, and new understandings. I am grateful for all of it. I want to finally acknowledge my darling wife Anna. Her love, support, encouragement, and, at times, patience have been unwavering. For that and for the loving home we have created I am eternally grateful.

This book is dedicated to those who have the courage to live in truth.

Planting the Seeds of Possibility

'There is my truth, your truth and the truth and none of them are right.' **Plato**

Welcome to the FreeMind Experience. My greatest hope is that you will read this book and be inspired to make the most of your precious life. Since the year 2000, I have dedicated myself to helping people find ways to live and love their lives to the full. I have worked with thousands of people in individual sessions, groups, workshops, conferences, and celebrations. During that time I have researched all sorts of different tools, techniques, and approaches – many of which I've trialed in the laboratory of my own life – to enable me to develop some simple and effective principles and practices that help people overcome their challenges, achieve their goals and enjoy more happiness and success in their lives.

I am absolutely in awe of humanity and fascinated with the power we have to change our lives in an instant. Every day I hear extraordinary stories of courage and resilience, and work with astounding people endeavoring to be their best and make the world a more beautiful place. However, many others are struggling against themselves, in conflict, frustrated, and afraid. Sometimes, despite their best efforts, they are not experiencing any real or lasting change.

The FreeMind Experience is a journey of self-discovery that involves learning to cherish and believe in yourself more. It is a way of nourishing yourself so that you can bring yourself into alignment with your greatest values and unleash your ultimate potential. However, it is not about sitting on top of a mountain meditating and only eating lentils, renouncing all worldly goods, and walking the earth barefoot. Instead, the FreeMind principles and practices combine the practical wisdom from the world's ancient traditions with the most effective rapid-behavior-change techniques – tried-and-tested tools, which anyone can learn to use and easily integrate into daily life to bring about real lasting change.

THE POWER TO CHANGE

Have you ever wondered what makes some people wake up on one day and decide to do something different with their lives? And what stops others from making the kinds of changes that they know will transform their lives for the better? Why do so many people knowingly block their own happiness on purpose?

Time and time again I have found, both in my Harley Street practice in London and working in the wider community, that many of our difficulties arise from unresolved fear and resistance; it blocks happiness and causes internal and interpersonal conflict. The process of human development from 'cradle to grave' seems to lead many of us to build up resentments, grudges, pains, and panics, which can end up skewing our feelings about ourselves and others. These fears make us ready to believe that we are not OK, that the world is not safe, and we must compete to survive. This combative stance with reality can underpin all human behaviors and feelings, and can really strip the joy from life. Freeing your mind from these feelings is what the FreeMind Experience is about.

This process starts by thinking about some big questions. For example, you might start by thinking about where you are in your life right now, and then asking yourself the following questions:

* Have you given up or dismissed a dream as being impossible?
* Are you truly being yourself in all that you do?
* Do you have total openness and honesty in all your relationships?
* What is that one thing you want to say to someone, but haven't yet found the courage to say?
* Are you excited by life?
* Are you resilient in the face of difficulty?
* Does your work reflect your highest ideals and your greatest potential?
* Are you totally in love with yourself?

Or, perhaps everything in your life is working well but you have an intuitive feeling that you have an untapped power waiting to be unleashed, a clarity aching to be expressed, a compassion waiting to be shared, extraordinary skills waiting to be crafted, a deeper peace and happiness waiting to be explored. So imagine for a moment what it would be to return to the very center of your being, and pull together the ashes of any forgotten dreams. To remember the echo of an ancient calling within you to make the most of this most exquisite life.

I have seen many people living out difficult and painful lives, who have forgotten the simple things that make living in this world worthwhile. Forgetting the richest joys that can be found in our deepest craving for awe and wonderment – the great adventure for true self-expression.

THE UNIVERSAL TRUTHS OF HAPPINESS

For many years I wasn't on a path of self-discovery. I wasn't a spiritual seeker – far from it. I was brought up a devout atheist, and had no leaning toward one school of thought over another. However, a truly life-changing event in 2000 inspired me to understand more about the human condition and our capacity to change. I'll describe this epiphany in the next chapter (see page 3) but when I had, what I now call that 'FreeMind Experience,' a deep sense of natural happiness welled up inside me and the course of my life changed in an instant. I was so inspired by the power of that moment of bliss, I devoted the rest of my life to researching and understanding how to be happy; and how to create paradigm-shifting experiences for others. To better understand contentment and the human condition, I studied the ancient and modern wisdom traditions, including philosophy, spirituality, theology, and psychology.

In that time, I discovered some amazing things about happiness, but I also became painfully aware that many schools of thought were dogmatic, prescriptive, and hypocritical, while many of the new-age type approaches were oversentimental and unscientific. I knew that many people are put off by that stuff, and it made me wonder how many people throw out the wisdom baby with the spiritual bathwater. The simple truth is that all these different models of happiness seem to say the same thing.

There is a more enlightened way of being that is full of peace, love and happiness.

Soon I noticed a number of other universal truths or principles, corroborated across different times and cultures, spiritual traditions and religions. These principles and practices go by many different names, in all sorts of different cultures and models, but they essentially seem to point to the same important truths.

1. There is a state of enlightenment that we can all connect to. This state of being is essentially a very powerful and peaceful mindset, which enables us to love ourselves, and others, unconditionally.

2. We connect to this state of enlightenment, or freedom, when we transcend our conditioned and limited sense of self (our ego). When we accept and love every part of

ourselves, and at the same time no longer identify with the fear and resistance of our personality, then we can experience real and lasting happiness.

3. Overcoming the fear and resistance of our personality involves some form of practice or process. Different cultures have very different ideas about this, but whether it is spinning like a whirling dervish, dancing tribally, praying, meditating or taking psychedelic plants in the jungle all of the wisdom traditions agree that transcendence involves some process of evolving our perspective beyond our limited sense of self.

4. There are ways of living together that support positive and unconditional ways of relating to each other so that we are more likely to be peaceful and happy. Loving communities built on principles of compassion, collaboration, non-competition, self-expression, creativity, and regular celebration help us to be happy.

From these four simple truths, I started to build the Three Pillars of FreeMind, which I'll share on pages xx–xxi, but first I had to discover the many reasons that make it more likely that we find it difficult to embrace these four simple truths and so struggle with life in some way.

WHY WE STRUGGLE

All the wisdom traditions clarify that living in a society that focuses on individualization, separation, and isolation is the quickest way to make everyone miserable. The Western model of civilization is a million miles from the enlightened description of how best to live together happily (see point 4 above).

What's more, our aggressive animal instincts and competitive social hierarchy means we are tuned to interpret reality from a fear-based survival perspective. In turn, this can lead us to see life as being, on the whole, threatening and challenging; and this fundamental resistance to life underpins all of our difficulties. It can lead us to believe that we are not OK, and that the world is hostile and dangerous. Situations start to occur whereby we start to say 'NO' to life and ourselves. I refer to these times as 'NO moments,' and over time they build up. We become more fearful, resistant, and judgmental; and our overall view of life can become negative.

Caught up in a NO state of fear and resentment, we block our happiness. For example, you may worry on some level about everything. You might be overly concerned about what others say, think, and do. Or maybe you don't notice any fear because you don't allow yourself to stop and feel anything. You may simply keep yourself busy all the time. Busyness is sometimes the best way of avoiding our doubts and fears. Or perhaps you never notice the degree to which fear impacts negatively on your life because you self-medicate by overeating, drinking, or taking pharmaceutical or recreational drugs.

When fear and resentment are running the show we are much more likely to harbor grudges and make judgments about other people. We are much more likely to fall out with friends and family members. Work is more likely to be a struggle, and we may be more likely to stress out about money when we don't have it – as well as more prone to stress about money when we have plenty of it. Going out may feel like

xvi THE FREEMIND EXPERIENCE

a threat or a chore because it is easier to avoid interaction. People become a nuisance to be gotten out of the way and, very often, we see others as simply a means to an end. The world becomes more competitive and aggressive, and we become more and more closed and hardened. Inevitably, this means avoiding real intimacy, and thereby living half-filled lives with half-told truths and half-lived dreams.

Where are you in this moment? Are you feeling fully expressed, vibrantly alive, and thrilled to be breathing each blessed breath? So many of us miss out on how amazing our lives could be because we compare ourselves to what we have known in the past or to others around us. However, what might happen if you compared your current reality to what you are truly capable of? If your greatest potential could speak to you now, who would it ask you to be? What else could you create, claim, and enjoy?

DROPPING RESISTANCE

Freeing your mind of all doubts, imagined inadequacies, grudges, and grumbles; letting go of your painful story, dropping your feelings of having been a victim, relaxing your need for control, and stopping trying to manipulate yourself and others is vital if you want to start enjoying life more. When we drop our resistance to life, even in the most difficult of times, we discover a huge capacity to be at peace. Developing that capacity to relax into the flow of life and to bring a deep and strongly held sense of YES to EVERYTHING is the secret. This is the foundation of the FreeMind Experience and the key to absolute happiness.

When we are free from over-identification with our aggrieved and resentful personal story, we can begin to relate more freely to every moment. Our potential is given the chance to truly shine through, and thus many of our limitations, which previously restricted us, dissolve. We become free in the moment and what usually erupts from us at that point is playful, positive, passionate, and alive. When we experience ourselves as whole and complete, and love ourselves unconditionally, we can finally let other people be who they truly are too. When we can love everyone else unconditionally, we become someone that brings out the very best in others. We become a blessing in our own lives and most certainly a blessing in the lives of others.

Absolute or unconditional happiness is the capacity to be at peace no matter what is going on around you. From that place you feel good because of who you are, not because of what you do or what you have. From this place you are not happy because x, y, and z have happened or because a, b, and c haven't happened. When you can free yourself, even just for a moment, from the idea that something external is the key to your happiness you begin to access a peace and contentment that dwarfs all your other experiences of contentment.

In my work, I have seen firsthand how the human mind battles to hold on to its resistance to life. It is difficult to relinquish the fight. It is not simple to relax and trust that all is well. When I am working with top achievers using advanced hypnotherapy techniques, speaking in schools to inspire children to engage in the world, or delivering values-based leadership training in Nigeria to reduce corruption, it is the same story. The human mind finds it very difficult to connect to the sense that everything is OK, and that we are complete and perfect. That part of our mind wants freedom, love, happiness, and contentment but the very nature of how it thinks makes all of those wonderful feelings much less likely to be experienced or lived fully on a long-term basis.

Getting over this general underlying resistance to life is a process of bringing a YES to what was previously a NO. The happiest person alive is the person who is most able to fully say 'YES' to what is happening in the moment. However, we can't do that until we are able to fully say 'YES' to ourselves – to be fully accepting and loving of ourselves as we are in that moment. However, to fully say 'YES' to ourselves, we have to be fully accepting, and in love with EVERYTHING that has ever happened to us.

This is what I call the 'FreeMind Triple YES.'

This is the path to total unconditional love and it is the foundation of ABSOLUTE HAPPINESS.

YES 1 You are fully at peace with everything that has ever happened to you.

YES 2 You are therefore fully at peace with who you are. You know that you are the perfect person in the perfect moment doing the perfect thing in absolutely the perfect way.

YES 3 You meet the present moment with a full and happy heart knowing that the universe and everything in it is happening in the perfect way at the perfect time.

The Three FreeMind Pillars and associated FreeMind Practices, which you'll discover in Part II of the book (from page 85), are designed to create a shift: from the resistant, fearful, and unhappy state of NO to the relaxed, loving, and happy state of YES. This is the FreeMind Experience and while living with that perspective permanently is nigh on impossible, learning to work with the practices suggested in this book makes life infinitely easier along the way.

THE THREE FREEMIND PILLARS OF PEACE, POWER, AND PURPOSE

Each of the FreeMind Pillars represents a whole range of principles and practices that enable a person to bring their deepest YES to life, and I have distilled them into these three key areas of understanding. Some of the materials are instructions to 'do' things differently. Other areas are more of an invitation to 'be' different. That is why I sometimes refer to the FreeMind Experience as 'the art and science of happiness.' By bringing together East and West, traditional and alternative, we meet on the solid ground of tried-and-tested principles and practices. I have seen these techniques work time and time again, and have helped thousands of people to transform their lives, and they work best when they follow this simple Three Pillar approach. By working in turn with each of the Three FreeMind Pillars and Practices, we begin to experience much more happiness and success in our lives. The process is summarized as follows:

PILLAR 1: FREEMIND PEACE

* **Deprogramming** is the first stage and involves dissolving, and letting go of all the thoughts, feelings, behaviors,

limited beliefs, and identities that are holding you back and skewing your perception of yourself and reality. Deprogramming is best summed up as unlearning old conditioning.

* This brings your deepest **peace** to life.
* The FreeMind Practice that makes this possible is **Emotional Intelligence.**
* When you have developed this practice you experience **GRATITUDE** for everything that has ever happened.

This is the **first YES** of the Triple YES.

PILLAR 2: FREEMIND POWER

* **Reprogramming** is the second stage and involves learning and practicing to relate to yourself and life in new ways. This is a process of reconditioning the mind, which enables you to change your life by changing your perceptions, expectations, and patterns of thought and speech, so that you can unleash your greatest potential. This is about bringing your mind, body, and soul into full alignment with fully empowered beliefs.
* Combining these new ways of being with the precision of taking definite actions with integrity, accountability, creativity, and efficiency brings your full **power** to life.
* The FreeMind Practice that makes this possible is **Success Psychology.**
* When you have developed this practice you experience **FULFILMENT** and things flow naturally in the best way possible.
* This is the **second YES** of the Triple YES.

PILLAR 3: FREEMIND PURPOSE

* **Reconnection** involves becoming aware of the deeper meaning of life within the context of interdependence and oneness. This is about being able to experience yourself as part of the singular field of reality. This sense of connection brings a happiness and joy to life that is contagious. Your joyful life will then become the most powerful inspiration for change in the lives of others. As your love and happiness lights up the world, you fulfill your purpose and your sense of connection to all things deepens. Everything becomes more meaningful, balanced, and beautiful.
* Reconnection is best summed up as living with **purpose** in your life.
* The FreeMind Practice that makes this possible is **Oneness Philosophy**.
* When you have developed this practice you experience **UNCONDITIONAL LOVE** for all things.
* This is the **third YES** of the Triple YES.

ONENESS

When we have a real and distinct sense of everything being interconnected and interdependent our life changes in profound ways. It is that vivid experience of oneness that enables us to relax fully in such a way that we get to experience absolute happiness. I'll describe how science has actually ratified the experience of oneness in Pillar 3 (see pages 184–9), but for now it is enough to say that it is about considering life from the perspective that everything happens in the perfect way at the perfect time. That is not a denial of what is difficult or challenging. It is not a happy Band Aid pasted over our troubles. It is simply a much wider view that can wrap its loving arms around absolutely everything. From there our battle with life dissolves like a sliver of tin in a furnace of a much deeper understanding. This more universal perspective is peaceful, powerful, and purposeful. It is the bedrock of enlightenment.

The key to happiness is moving from identifying with our small, personal, limited, and fearful personality, and identifying more with our larger, impersonal, unlimited, and loving universality.

If you already see the world through that lens then hopefully this book will serve to refresh what you already know to be true in your heart. However, if any of the ideas are new for you, then I would like to suggest that you start from the position of being open to what I am saying while questioning everything. All our problems are due to us being too rigid in our beliefs, so I invite you to explore all of this from a position of total uncertainty. In exactly the same way, I ask you also to imagine that some of what you currently believe is also possibly limited and inaccurate.

Imagine for a moment that you are as deluded as I must be in some way ... Be open to a world of possibility without being certain about anything. Let us look together at how and why we get separated from a simpler, more enlightened way of being and how we can so easily struggle along our way.

Journey with me into the heart of what it is to be fully human, with all of our paradoxical openings and closings. With our propensity to fly high and then crash hard, our wanting to be connected, and our fear of being trapped. Let's look at our inherent love of truth and freedom and our inability at times to take a real stand for ourselves; why fear sometimes prevents us from being the incredible person that our heart longs for us to be; and how freeing our mind helps us move beyond our problems.

FINDING PERFECTION IN EVERYTHING

Many traditional schools of thought, therapy, psychology, and medicine come from the perspective of trying to fix problems. The FreeMind Experience is not about fixing problems. It is more a matter of embracing the total human journey, including our difficulties. As described above (see page xvi), it is about moving beyond all your negations, freeing yourself of all your resistances, and coming into a state of ultimate YES with all that has brought you into this moment. Being at peace with the world as you find it. Loving the way you find yourself. Seeing the beauty in all challenges, the potential growth in difficult situations, and holding space for all of your paradoxes and conflicts.

FreeMind is about being beyond the idea that freedom is escape from the storm – the fantasy of never-ending peace, but rather knowing that it is about experiencing peace within the storm. To see that enlightenment is not the end of our neuroses. It is simply being open to the entirety of your experience, wrapping every aspect of yourself – including your challenges – in love, certain in the knowledge that everything that happens, plays a vital part in the unfolding of what is supposed to happen.

Once we experience that unconditional love for ourselves, we naturally want to contribute, collaborate, and engage with others in more loving and playful ways. In turn, this brings even more gratitude, fulfillment, and unconditional love to life. From there we experience absolute happiness. We are naturally much more wonderful to be around and our life begins to reflect and amplify the love that we are giving and receiving more freely.

When we get that, we also realize that:

Life is perfect!

When we get that we realize that:

There is nothing wrong with you. [*]

Or put another way:

You are perfect in every way. [†]

---

[*] Not even a little bit.
[†] Especially including all the bits that seem to hold you back.

Finally, to see a short welcome video visit www. freemindproject/welcome or scan the QR code below.

Here you can also download a free preparatory hypnosis recording that will make this book more engaging and enjoyable. This book is not designed to be just an intellectual learning experience. It is a very real invitation for you to enjoy more happiness and success in your life. Using hypnosis and the support videos whilst you read this book will make the whole experience much more likely to be truly transformational.

PART I

AWAKENING TO THE FREEMIND EXPERIENCE

'Life can only be understood backwards, but it must be lived forwards.'

Søren Kierkegaard

CHAPTER 1

The Beginning of FreeMind

The simple truth is that I feel incredibly lucky to have been blessed with a chance encounter with the right person at exactly the right moment in my life. The experience led me to devote my life to developing the FreeMind Practices and then helping others to find their happiness too. In sharing my story, I hope you'll see that part of the process is about being open to change. At that time, I was perfectly ready to think and feel differently. I just didn't know it. And this makes me curious about where you are in your life and intrigued about all the different things that have led you to be reading this line of text right now. Perhaps you are ready too? Maybe you want to enjoy more peace, power, and purpose in your life. The smallest shift can make the world of difference. It can happen in an instant.

A PERFECT MOMENT

Before my epiphany in 2000, I wasn't driven by any sense of purpose, other than the desire to pursue and experience pleasure. I had never connected to any passion for learning and tried very hard to do the absolute minimum in every area of life. Nothing inspired me and my willingness to apply myself was woefully absent. Underneath this very laidback exterior, I know now that I was being held back by some of the classic fears of the personality (my ego). People choose different ways of managing those fears. Some people are pushed on by it and, as a result, go on to do great things with their lives. It didn't turn out that way for me. Underneath it all, I was petrified that I wasn't good enough. Deep down I was afraid that if I did try hard, nothing good would come of it and I would have to witness myself being a failure. Instead, I chose to believe that I was great and never put myself 'out there' to be tested. In order to make that delusional waltz workable, I chose to look for the reasons in everyday life that justified why I didn't want to engage in 'normal' life.

Being a teenager in the 1980s meant I didn't have to look very hard. At that time, there seemed to be a wholesale move toward a set of values that made less and less sense to my heart. Everyone seemed to get busier and less content. My friends and I would see our parents coming home from work tired, stressed, and dissatisfied. As far as I could see, very few people were especially happy. This didn't make me want to engage in life and, what's more, I didn't have any idea about what I wanted to do with my life. It seemed crazy to me that what we study in school as kids, what exams we take in our teenage years, lay the foundations for our adult careers and have a huge impact on our ability to enjoy a full and rounded life. Perhaps you chose well and have landed in exactly the right career or perhaps with hindsight you might have made a few changes – not listened to others, been more careful about the limiting train tracks that you were laying down for yourself. Well, at the time, it seemed insane to me and I saw the whole prospect of engaging in life, in this way, as dangerous.

I realize now, that I had a deep desire for self-expression and autonomy that I simply wasn't in a position to enjoy. I wasn't consciously aware of those frustrations at the time. All I knew was that I wanted to go out and have fun. I wanted to avoid being inculcated or dragged down by any kind of thinking, which would lead me to accept that life had to be a certain kind of way. I was scared to try. I was scared to fail. And yet, I was also acutely aware how easily I could get pulled into a world and a way of thinking that would take me further away from real happiness.

IN THE PURSUIT OF FREEDOM

Happiness and pleasure became my only interests. I shunned the everyday 'rat race,' and became committed to finding freedom. I wasn't alone in my thinking. Turns out there were lots of us that wanted no part of that 'normal' everyday world either, and this wholesale disenfranchisement fueled the dance revolution that swept through the UK. It began in the late 1980s and by the early 1990s there were literally millions of people going out every weekend to dance and celebrate a different way of living. It was during that time that I first experienced feeling unconditional love for someone who wasn't a family member. Dancing at huge events, moving in synchrony with thousands of other people, gave me my first experience of tribalism. As the music shifted and changed, we moved in unison, enjoying in harmony, and gasping at times together as an amazing piece of music was offered up. Smiles, laughter, and pleasure rippled through the crowd as a unified whole. Judgments dissolved, affection shared, people were connected by the very virtue of sharing that experience together. In that space, your heart can't help but remember the naturalness of feeling a loving connection to your fellow humans. In that space, you move, think, and feel as one, and it feels really good. I now understand that those shared and synchronized experiences gave me my first taste of the joy of the oneness perspective.

It was my love for these extraordinary feelings and unconscious remembrances that took me to the place where the best parties in the world were happening. In January 1992, I went to north Goa in India where I discovered a profound understanding of what it is to be truly free and happy and how, when we are in our most alive place, we can powerfully bring other people back to life too. I fell in love with partying in such a way that I became involved in the production of these events. However, what began as an earnest desire to bring love to life through the creation of life-affirming celebrations, turned, over the years, into unbridled hedonism. My love of freedom and its attendant rejection of the 'everyday' world began as a pursuit of happiness but soon were marred by all manner of darkness and difficulties that grumbled underneath all of my seeming enjoyments. Resistance, resentments, and judgments began to build up and I had to defend against them.

I came to love the glamor and glory of the dark underbelly of the underground party world. It felt like a rebellion but it was all about consumption and excess. My sense of humor was addictively dark. This, I see now, was a huge defense. Cynicism protected me from the horror of what I saw happening in my heart and the revulsion at what I saw in the world. Nothing made sense. There was no purpose to life. It seemed to me that the only thing worth doing well was using the senses we had been given to give ourselves colorful and exciting experiences. The richest tastes, the sweetest and loudest sounds, the most sumptuous touches, the latest nights, the most glamorous parties, the seediest sexual encounters.

In the indulgence there was freedom. There was escape. There was a rejection of law, order, and ordinariness. We wanted to be beyond social convention but in doing so forgot the point of the game. I now see that in the search for hedonistic obliteration there is a deeper hankering to escape the rigid and limited personality. Have you ever noticed that craving for obliteration? Felt a yearning for a complete merging or dissolution? A moment of fearless bliss? How has it expressed itself? When you have wanted to be free from fear, having fun, feeling alive what, if anything, have you reached for? What have you needed or wanted to help you let go? Underneath that desire for freedom, what part of you was actually seeking something beautiful and true? Sometimes it is not so much about escape. It is in fact much more about a sense of connection — a dissolving into something much bigger and wider. As you are reading these words now, take a moment to notice that part of you craving an opportunity for a pure moment of total free self-expression and connection. In my past, without even realizing that was what I was looking for, I was searching for that in all the wrong places.

AWAKENING

After eight years of working as an event organizer and party promoter, I returned to India for the millennium celebration. At that time, I believed I was truly living a free life and didn't expect for a minute what I was about to learn about REAL freedom. India bringing me in close, slowly shaking her head, gently sweeping the hair from my eyes, stroking my cheek, and whispering to me softly 'close my darling.'

It was New Year's Eve 1999, the biggest most significant calendar date of my life, and the roads were alive with motorbikes, tearing through the night like maniacal mosquitoes — everyone desperate for a historically good time. In the early 1980s I remember listening to the Prince song '1999,' and thinking what a party that would be. And here it was, the biggest New Year's Eve party ever. After looking around, my good friend Piers and I selected an outdoor party at the hilltop enclosure at Vagator.

It was perfect. There was a huge dance floor surrounded on all sides by a large chill-out area punctuated with trees. The area was flooded with the purple hue of ultraviolet light and huge canvasses of beautiful ultraviolet art hung between the trees and above the speakers, inviting you into fantasy spacescapes and fluorescent classic Indian spiritual imagery. Wool had ingeniously been dipped in fluorescent paint and strands stretched as lasers cutting across the perfumed night sky, or they had been crisscrossed as mathematical sculptures of vectors, fractals, and cradles. The sound system was sumptuous, crisp, and incredibly loud. The chill-out area consisted of 30 or 40 chai mats, each with its own chai mama sat in the middle, brewing up her own recipe of delicious chai tea. The air was rich with the heavenly scent of cinnamon, cardamom, ginger, cloves, and masala spices. Intermittently one or other would stoke up her little hot-bellied paraffin burner, lighting up her miniature empire with a rich orange glow as flames escaped and wildly cupped their blackened tin kettles. Everything was in place. It was a thunderous party full of much wonderment and joy. We, along with 2,000 others, started dancing, moving in unison, stirring ourselves into a throbbing throng of ecstatic revelation and expansion. We were entering a world of dance and delirium and were being woven into a sea of wonderful madness.

The stranger that changed my life managed to do so without uttering a word. I realize now that I was wonderfully open and ready for change but I had no idea that something so simple at the right time could have such an impact. He was a very skinny Indian Swami — a wandering holy man — all bones at angles wrapped in two cloths: one dusty claret red, and the other an aging mustard yellow. His long hair was dark, and gray in places, with part of it tied in a messy knot on top of his head while the rest fell about his shoulders and caught in his straggly beard. At first glance, his sinewy and weathered exterior made him look old but he was actually fairly young.

He was still and utterly serene, which made me wonder what he was doing there and what on earth he thought of the writhing party scene before him. I didn't dwell on it but noticed he was still there when the sun came up. I kept dancing all that day till night fell again. I did toy with the idea of going for a double sunrise, but by 11pm, after 18 hours of dancing, I was utterly spent. I stumbled back to the hotel, and fell into bed expecting to sleep forever. Strangely, however, I woke about five hours later feeling refreshed, present, and incredibly happy. In the distance, I was surprised to hear the thumping heartbeat of the party still going. It was now January 2nd and people were still partying! I was hungry and wanted breakfast but it was too early, so I decided to find out who could still be dancing.

There were maybe 30 or 40 people dancing and another 100 or so reclining on various chai mats. The atmosphere didn't really compare to New Year's Eve but it still felt good. With a smile, I looked around the party and there I saw the Baba – the holy man. He was still there! It didn't look like he had moved. Watching him from a short distance away, I noticed that he was striking looking and had an incredibly feline energy about him. Seated in a yoga-like position, he took his time bringing his hair, his beard, and his blanket robes into order by stroking them straight with his hands working like licked-wet paws. This grooming and self-gathering process was slow and seemed ritualistic. I was captivated by his energy and felt compelled to go and speak to him but was held back by a powerful, if very subtle, sense that there was some deeper purpose to this encounter – and that something of importance was about to happen. This intuitive awareness was a new sensation for me, so before going over there I took a moment to savor the experience, so as to discern what it actually might mean. Leaning into that intuition was a moment of uncommon introspection for me that made all of the difference to the outcome. I noticed just how much shallowness was operating in me and chose to do something different for a change.

'Oh, I know...' piped up part of me, 'Go over there and talk about Buddhism with him.' I had a brief image of myself deeply impressing this holy man with my proudly atheistic, yet deeply aware, grasp on consciousness. I imagined easily the surprise and the respect he would afford me when I shared my 'dazzlingly' insightful ideas with him. Fortunately somewhere, deep down, I knew that THAT was not what this was about. (I am now also very aware that my original and limited grasp on Buddhism would not have roused much interest or respect from him.)

So, I continued to lean against my tree and ponder. 'Oh I know, maybe he will see right into my soul and tell me something I need to know ...' Also tempting, but I didn't feel at that moment as if I wanted to know something. I wasn't searching and thought my well-established form of godless, egocentric hedonism was serving me fairly well, so I didn't have any questions that were alive for me at that time. So, that didn't make me go over there either. I was about to ponder on, when a somewhat wiser and seemingly less patient part of myself suggested fairly loudly in my interior world, 'Why don't you just go over there and see what happens?' That felt right, and so that is what I did.

As I sat down, he said hello to me in that beautiful Indian way, by ever so slightly wobbling his head and smiling at me. I smiled back. I smiled at the chai mama too and ordered some tea, but surprisingly her welcome was not so warm. She seemed a little distressed. The chai mama handed me my chai and I sat there wondering why I had thought that there was something 'special' meant to happen. I chose to simply relax and enjoy my tea. Moments later, the chai mama started talking to the Swami in Hindi. She was clearly upset and was being really gnarly. Most people treat these wandering holy men with great respect, but not her, not on that day at least. Her tone was getting more and more exasperated and strident. He remained calm and silent throughout, which seemed to be driving her crazier.

I gleaned from the exchange that he had consumed a number of teas and hadn't yet paid. He listened to her, waited for a pause in her tirade, and then just very purposefully wobbled his head and smiled warmly. This time, the wobble didn't say 'hello.' It appeared to silently say, 'All will be well. Trust me.' She snorted through her nostrils and went about stoking her fire. I wondered how many times he had reassured her in that way.

There are approximately 15 million of these wandering holy men (and women) in India. Having given up property and worldly goods, they walk in faith that if they are in alignment with the universe, they will be provided for. The idea is that owning property or possessions makes you fearful and also forces you into being a political being. Your things start to own you and it becomes difficult to be totally truthful with everyone about everything. You have to hold down a job and play the game. These wandering mendicants are free of that. The idea of them walking around with a begging bowl is somewhat of a misnomer. They shouldn't have to beg. Truth-sayers, they are powerful people in alignment with the divine universe. If they wander into the village, it is a blessing and they are usually welcomed because of what they have to say. In exchange, they are given food and shelter. They walk in service. They walk in faith that if they are giving, they will receive all that they require.

I had heard about these renunciants and, while I loved the idea and their willingness to live in accordance with these principles, I thought it was an insane way to live. As I sat next to him, I contemplated this, and then suddenly it hit me. I knew exactly what I was there for. There was not one iota of doubt in my mind. This was a new feeling but my whole body rang true with absolute certainty. No question. No quibble. Not one flicker of resistance. I was there to pay for his tea.

THE DIVINE INTERCONNECTION OF EVERYTHING

I was right all along. It wasn't about me: it was neither about impressing him with my knowledge, nor him looking into my eyes and imparting some great truth. I was simply there as part of the divine balancing force field; to ensure he was provided with what he needed. It felt so clear and so right, I immediately proceeded to get my money out. However, very suddenly I felt conscious that I didn't want praise from him. I didn't want this to be about 'me' doing something generous for him. It really wasn't about me, and so I subtly prepared a little care package for him with enough money to pay for about 20 teas. I then secreted it under one of the folds of his blanket while he was looking in the other direction. I placed it in a way where it couldn't be missed and he would find it very soon. I paid for my own tea and walked off without even saying goodbye. As I walked away, I was flooded with a sense of perfection; a rush of YES energy went through my whole body. I vibrated with a kind of universal THANK YOU. Divine order had prevailed and I was its instrument. This was evidence – real hard evidence – of this beautiful principle:

If you live for truth and love,
you will be provided for.

I was blessed to have been in the right headspace at the right time, and in the right place so that I perceived reality in this way at that moment. It felt like everything in my life had brought me to that moment to have that experience. A deep-seated feeling began to erupt through my spine and I knew I had to get out of there. I didn't want to block this feeling but I was starting to feel incredibly emotional and then I heard her ... A beautiful loving female voice inside my mind-body inviting me to see that everything that I had ever been afraid of was a total waste of time. She whispered that I had made my life so difficult with all of that running around. 'You are safe and loved,' she said and, with that, I broke open. My eyes filled with tears, a huge lump appeared in my throat and I rushed out of there.

I didn't feel fit for public consumption. Breakfast could wait. What's more, I didn't want to squash these feelings or be judged for them. Dead ahead was Vagator Hill and I intuitively knew that's where I had to be, so I jumped on my bike and rode as far up the dirt track as I could, before leaning the motorbike against the hill and scrambling the final 130 feet or so on foot, to the top. It was a glorious day, with a platinum-blue sky and, to the left, a huge view of the

Vagator sea line. The cliff tops bordered by a palm tree forest. I was now free to feel fully what was happening. I sat down, and a deep joy welled up inside me and a deep vibration of a hugely relaxing YES moved through me. Amid these feelings of wanton abandon and exaltation was an intense happiness, the like of which I had never experienced before. At exactly the same time, the deepest most painful sadness and grief coursed through every fragment of my being. A dark sorrow for all the pain I had caused myself by pointlessly imagining there was something wrong. I was in a divine universe of love. With this awareness I dissolved into the physical sensations and I melted further into the experience and my surroundings.

In that one moment, I felt connected to everything and everyone that had ever existed. My sense of 'I' was now a sense of all. There was a continuous sensation of oneness and unity with everything that stretched in every direction simultaneously. There was no here and there, no then and now. It was perfect. Everything was perfect. I therefore was, and always had been, perfect. In that moment, I sensed that all of the world's struggles and all of human suffering (like my own) were driven by our imaginary idea of separation and our pressured need to therefore survive.

All my suffering and seeming dysfunction was simply a reflection of a set of inaccurate ideas, which I had been holding on to (unknowingly), and that were throwing me off balance. That imbalance made me behave in (fearful) ways that prevented me from feeling the full force of bliss and perfection that I was feeling in that divine moment.

In that experience of clarity, with those limited ideas at least on hold, I felt the joyful perfection of the universe coursing through all the fibers, sinews, forests, mountains, and oceans of my extended universal being. I was not part of the universe. There was no separation anymore. I was the universe. What was exquisitely magical was the familiarity I felt at that moment. I was finally home. That was so telling. I knew this place at my core – it was me. Not that other guy. Here I knew that everything was in its place. I could see and feel into the darker warrior energy of human behaviors, and I could feel the sense of separation and incumbent powerlessness driving all of the pointless suffering in the world.

In that moment, I realized that everything was truly OK. Everything had always been OK. I finally understood what the world's religions and spiritual traditions had been attempting to explain. I didn't suddenly believe in an external and separate divinity but I did feel deeply connected to a perfect consciousness. In that moment I understood all religious descriptions of reality to be impossible attempts to put into words the experience of connected wonderment that comes from the awareness of the intrinsic interconnectedness of everything. That is God – and it is not jam-packed full of love. It *is* LOVE. Beyond the realm of the afraid-ego personality there is a total loving peace.

The sense of relief was so profound that a deep laugh erupted uncontrollably out of me and I laughed harder than I ever have before, and at exactly the same time I wept inconsolably with the deepest waves of grief and compassion. Howling with laughter and wailing with grief, alone on top of one of the most beautiful hills in the world surrounded by sea and color. I disappeared into the experience completely. I melted flat down onto the ground and let it all in and let it all out. This was the sweetest moment of my life and I still feel the shock waves in my now open heart. I am sure by many peoples' perspective, it would have looked as if I were having a complete and utter breakdown. I guess that is what it was – a total breakdown of an idea, of a position, of a worldview.

What I experienced was clear and pure, complete and perfect. It totally changed my life in an instant. As the waves of my epiphany began to settle and my sense of self began to reappear, I got to my feet and looked at the extraordinary beauty of the Indian landscape all around me. Everything bristled with life. Every particle of everything was vibrating and alive including every one of my cells. I saw magic every- where and I then noticed a gentle breeze flowing up the hill. I turned to follow the wind as it moved past me, moving up into the crystalline blue sky above the hill. There my eyes happened upon a glorious scene. Playing above me were seven eagles. I didn't know how long they had been there but they felt like my witnesses. The love I felt for them in that moment surged through me without boundary. I felt part of them and they felt like an auspicious sign from the universe that something extraordinary had just happened. I then noticed they seemed to be playing some kind of game.

A smile of wonderment slowly opened through me in amazement as I realized that the game involved trying to take a small twig away from each other. It was like watching the most exquisite fighter-plane tag team duel; only they were much better flyers. My jaw dropped as they barreled into each other, turning and twisting to escape with the much- prized twig intact. This was all happening between about 15 and 25 feet off the ground. Then one eagle in a rather over-zealous attempt to steal the twig crashed into another and the twig was dropped and began to fall to the ground.

Stunned, I watched one of them fold itself into a tight ball and plummet to the ground, as if as heavy as lead. At first I thought it had been hurt in the collision but then, just as it was about to hit the ground, it caught level with the falling twig. In an instant, it unfolded the full glory of its wings, snatched the twig in its beak, and twisted and banked hard, managing with no time to spare, to soar back into the air totally victorious. It flew above its compadres and I swear I could hear them all applauding. I certainly was. I had never seen such mastery.

This bird was in full command of its skill. It was a golden moment that immediately smacked me with its relevance. They were playing. They were having fun. They were, of course, also practicing their most vital survival skill. It was exactly this deft ability that enables this bird to feed itself. What it loved to do was what it was best at – that is how it earned its living. This was its very nature. Because it loves playing that game, it practices and practices and practices until it has turned that natural ability into an absolute art form. In that moment my old career died. I wanted that kind of a job. I wanted to find work that brought my nature to life. I wanted to find work that to me was like playing. I wanted to be so lost in the joy of my work that the idea of it as work would fall away, and what was left would feel like a sense of me simply being myself and finding a way to eat through that process. I wanted to be free to be totally myself. I sensed that if I could rest in that nature everything would be fine. I would catch the twig. I would fly into the sky free and victorious with everything that I needed. This, for me, was the beginning of my true purpose – my passion and love for helping others enjoy their own FreeMind Experience.

The interconnected sense of perfection that I experienced in Goa inspired me to transform my life and it still informs everything that I do today. On that same day I sent my business partner an email and told him that my days as a club and party promoter were over. I told him that I realized that what I thought was happiness was not anywhere close to what is actually possible. I was clear that my old life was built on principles and practices that were taking me further away from my ability to enjoy life. So, it simply had to stop. That clarity felt so good because it made it easy. There is something amazing about one day saying enough is enough. Although I had no idea what I was going to do, taking a stand for my real happiness felt immediately good.

As soon as I got back home from India I sold my house, bought a smaller one, paid off all of my debts, and threw myself into learning. I had never cared about learning before. Well, now I did. I had a voracious appetite. I knew that I wanted to learn everything I could about happiness and how epiphanies could be created. I wanted to know where this experience of perfect bliss and awareness had come from. I wanted to know how to stay close to it. I wanted to know how I had changed and why I had changed. I could map so many of the little thoughts and ideas that were in my mind beforehand that made it happen. I was totally captivated by the idea that surely it is possible to line up these ideas, to organize a set of worldview-changing concepts, theories, and perceptions so that maybe I could help other people see the world as a beautiful, loving, and perfect place.

What could you choose for yourself today? What gifts could be found in doing something different? Maybe that's changing careers? Maybe that's walking away from friendships that no longer inspire or nourish you? Maybe that's simply dumping your TV in the garbage or agreeing to never reading another (fear- and fantasy-peddling) magazine ever again. In my work helping people to have FreeMind Experiences it amazes me how, underneath it all, their heart knows exactly what to do. Yes, it can take courage to take those vital steps toward real self-expression and freedom, but your heart knows exactly what is calling you forward. You know exactly what would serve you to move beyond. As scary as those first steps can be, they are also immediately joyful.

CHAPTER 2

Bringing FreeMind
to the World

Throwing myself into study was a truly exciting time in my life. Everything I learned confirmed what I knew in my heart to be true. During this time, I discovered hypnotherapy as an incredible tool for connecting people to their natural happiness. I didn't study hypnotherapy to become a therapist but knew that trance or meditation seemed to sit in the middle of many other approaches, which are able to help people think and feel differently. The popularity of stage hypnotism shows means that some people (including myself originally) have some strange ideas about hypnosis. It looks as if the hypnotist is wielding power over the person. However, most of the time these shows are more about a certain kind of person really loving the opportunity to entertain a crowd. The hypnosis simply takes away their fear and empowers them to be silly and have fun. They get lots of applause and appreciation, and so it continues from there. So what looks like control is more a matter of the hypnotist giving permission and setting the stage for extroverts to enjoy being the center of attention.

Actually we all go in and out of hypnotic states every day. It is a natural state of entrancement most usually experienced first thing in the morning and last thing at night. Daydreaming, or being lost in thought, also induces this natural hypnotic state. Some people call it being a million miles away. Anyone who drives may also have experienced it when they have been driving back home on autopilot – totally unaware of the process of driving. We pull into the driveway with hardly any memory of how we got there.

In the simplest of terms hypnosis is basically a very deep state of relaxation. When we are relaxed we are essentially less fearful. Once fear and resistance is reduced it is possible to think more positively and powerfully about what is possible. In hypnosis, or deep relaxation, it is possible to be a lot more objective about who you are and how you are behaving. From there, it is possible to identify with more effective ways of being. I truly believe that everyone should be taught self-hypnosis and the power we have to change our thoughts, feelings, and behaviors. I especially believe that it should be taught in schools. That is probably one of the simplest ways to make the biggest changes in our world.

Talking therapies work at the level of the conscious mind, which can take a very long time to create change. Unlike hypnosis, metaphor, and music, which bypass that process and work much more rapidly by making powerful changes at the unconscious level. So by combining the FreeMind Pillars and Practices with hypnosis and music, I have created ways of inducing FreeMind Experiences in other people. This is what my private practice revolves around.

This is in stark contrast to the standard approach to health and mental wellbeing. The principles of traditional hypnotherapy, psychology, and psychiatry are based on the idea that people have problems and therapy helps to glue them back together, so they can return to the treadmill of life. Of course, there are some incredibly enlightened practitioners, but many simply operate on the inbuilt assumption that 'out there' is OK, and we have to help people become more fully formed individuals, who can then integrate fully into our 'wonderful' civilized (*ahem*) world. However, in my experience, those people most afflicted with psychological challenges and emotional difficulty are those who have enough awareness to see that much of the civilized world is built on values that are destructive, debilitating, and depressing.

When Mahatma Gandhi was asked about Western civilization. He said, 'I think it would be a good idea.'

However, if you believe, as I do, that everything is in place, and everything is as it should be, why would someone feel bad or anxious? So, when I started in private practice, I focused on exploring what would happen if, instead of gluing people's egos back together, I helped them recognize that their ego was a fear-handling mechanism that often ended up making them more afraid, unhappier, and less free. And the results were amazing. Rapidly I began to see that many of my clients who presented with depression or anger issues were actually having a healthy reaction to an unhealthy world. In the same way that not drinking enough water can result in a headache then, as unpleasant as that headache is, it is simply a product of not drinking enough water. The headache is evidence that the system works. The headache is a message, an invite, or a reminder to drink more water.

In the same way, people are not depressed due to an imbalance of chemicals in the brain. They have an imbalance of chemicals in their brain *due* to being depressed. This may sound like a small detail, but it is a fundamentally different way of looking at our emotions and how best to treat them. If feelings of depression, anxiety, guilt, shame, fear, or self-doubt are as yet unheard messages, then why would we want to silence what they have to say? Yes, we can replace those chemicals and the sadness and difficulty may be reduced, or may even go away completely, but would we imagine that is a good thing? Surely, this approach simply lets people get on with their unsatisfying lives without noticing their dissatisfaction. That might sound like a good thing, but I know that if my life was depressing or made me feel anxious and stressed, then I would rather know about it, so that I could do something about it.

Our emotions are amazing internal guidance mechanisms that help us work out who we are, where we are, where we will work at our best, who will be good for us, and what do to with this precious life.

BRINGING ABOUT CHANGE

The FreeMind Experience can help you find the clarity and courage to feel into your emotions, to listen to them, to clear out all of your old pain and resentments, and then to get a clean reading on where you are today. As you work your way through the three Pillar Practices in Part II (see pages 115, 165, and 223), you'll find your emotional awareness increases to give you better insights, and a deeper understanding of what your heart is trying to tell you – emotional outbursts are not random, they come from somewhere. Yes, some people do discover that they need to leave their current job, or partner, or make some other significant life change, but many others realize that it is less about changing things and more a matter of committing fully to their work and their relationships so they can start enjoying them again. In other words, it is less about making external changes and more about opening up to intimacy or connecting more deeply with yourself, your relationships, or your work.

I have helped many people realize that their depression is a part of them: an alert telling them, 'Enough is enough, I have had it with you going out into the world with these ideas and feelings that are holding you back.' Depression closes down the body and zaps energy. However, feeling down or depressed is actually a totally appropriate response and presents an opportunity to evaluate our values and beliefs. To perhaps see how they are leading us to live in ways that aren't really in keeping with our heart, our potential, or our highest ideals. This is also true of the world, or our national economy when it is depressed. It is an opportunity for us to take stock and look again at our social values. To ask, 'How did we collectively get here? How would we like to proceed?' These are important questions – and, yes, the answers might be difficult to hear and the transitions may well be challenging – but these messages are a truth waiting to be understood.

The FreeMind Experience is about seeing everyone and everything as whole, complete, and perfect including all our challenges, and then creating the loving context, which makes change much more likely. In practice, I have found that years of dysfunction and difficulty can be resolved incredibly quickly – so rapidly, in fact, that my respect for the power of the unconscious mind is boundless. To be clear, the FreeMind Experience is not a cure, it is simply a tool to be used to access that place in ourselves where we remember that our true nature is a connected part of a singular field of wondrous perfection. From there, there is no problem to be fixed and new more-aligned behaviors evolve naturally. All our challenges can be seen as part of how we have been trying to help ourselves. When those defensive parts of ourselves are loved, we become much more able and open to change.

Using the FreeMind Practices in Part II, it's possible to change many challenges and difficult behaviors. However, almost everyone has some sticking patterns that may prove much harder to shift; I believe we are meant to have some perfect flaws. So if your hope is that through this work, you'll end up in some place totally free of challenges and fears, then you'll be missing the point of the experience. Sometimes our freedom is felt most keenly when we are able to love the most challenging aspects of ourselves. It is through loving every part of ourselves that we see the divine perfection in all things. Remembering that is not always easy, but when you are open to what is happening and love it, trusting that everything is working out perfectly, you open to life in ways that make it infinitely more enjoyable and exciting.

We don't overcome resistances by letting them go, ignoring them, or by dismissing them as unspiritual, but by loving every aspect of our experience, including our fears and resentments. When you have the courage to journey into the heart of your most painful emotions and your most rigid resistances, then you'll be able to bring love and light into the darkest corners of your life. There you'll discover who you truly are. In that place you are furnished with all the understanding and compassion you require to make the most of your precious life.

All of our difficult emotions are our signposts to freedom. Don't ignore them; listen to them and amplify them. They are an invitation from your heart to come home.

OUR RELATIONSHIP WITH NO

I have helped many people discover where their general resistance to life comes from, and there seem to be a number of classic moments in our development that can lead to a build up of negative feelings about ourselves and the world. While everyone is different, of course, these key moments seem to be poignant for most people. Not all of these NO moments will immediately resonate with you, and some may seem like small details, but over the years they often accumulate to create ways of thinking, feeling, and behaving that make it harder for us to be happy.

Think about for it a moment ... How does it feel when you let fear control your choices? It's likely that you experience a feeling of contracting and pulling back. Fear can prevent you from taking those courageous steps that will enable you to enjoy life and love to the full. You might experience it as feeling like a slight coolness – a sensibility that is somewhat practical but also a little frail – a polite quietness that shrinks and sits back down. Our light flickers and then dies down bit by bit. We feel safer and yet somehow sadder at the same time. Transforming your response to these NO moments is critical to the process of freeing your mind. Leaving them unresolved allows fear and resistance to rule, which in turn blocks our natural state of happiness and success.

THE CLASSIC RESULTANT BELIEFS

In psychology, these challenging moments in our development are well documented. In my practice, day in and day out, I see these key moments as having a negative influence on people's ability to be happy. This leads to a set of universal limiting beliefs that can really hold people back. Negative as these beliefs appear to be, they are generated to help us feel in control. They are created by the mind to help us make sense of the perceived threat and are designed to support us. Unfortunately, as we get older, these protective belief systems continue and can potentially end up limiting us terribly.

Most people are not aware that they are being held back by these fears because we usually don't spend too much time examining our doubts. However, it is incredibly liberating to meet with these beliefs and dissolve them with gratitude and love. Trusting that these limiting beliefs were once an act of self-love is a vital part of the process. That can be challenging because these classic limiting beliefs can result in pushing away opportunity, sabotaging love, and avoiding real intimacy. But love is the only thing that will help them transform into more beautiful beliefs.

The classic driving fears of the personality are:

* I'm not good enough.
* I don't belong.
* I am on my own.
* The world can't give me what I need.
* It's all pointless anyway.
* I must cover up my true nature.
* Don't stand out.
* No one ever truly understands me.

These fears can end up producing a whole range of compensatory behaviors that prevent people from enjoying their lives. Typically these would be:

* I must control myself.
* I must control others.
* I must present myself in certain ways.
* I must make lots of money.
* Material things will save me.
* I must compete.

* I must compare myself to others to see my value.
* I am not OK, unless someone else says so.
* Don't let people in.
* Don't share myself completely.
* Only love people with whom I feel safe.
* There isn't enough for everyone.
* Hold back.
* Don't give too much away.
* Only when I am rich and famous will I be OK.
* I must do something historically significant with my life.
* I must make a difference.

The FreeMind Practices can help connect us to a more peaceful positive state of being where we feel part of the wider universe. From there we can easily dissolve the limiting beliefs of the ego-personality, stop the associated compensatory, destructive, and isolating behaviors, and then bring the most joyful, brilliant, and loving versions of ourselves back to life.

If you believe you are separate you will imagine you are inadequate. Then you will most likely behave like an idiot. If you run around like an idiot, things will not go well for you. Heaven and hell are available right now. You decide in every moment. Every situation is an opportunity born out of love or fear.

CHAPTER 3

The Classic NO Moments: Fear and Resistance from the Very Beginning

Not long ago I watched some clips from the 'Ironman' competition. This extreme triathlon involves swimming 2.4 miles in open water (much harder than a swimming pool), cycling 112 miles and then running a full 26.2-mile marathon. The footage was extraordinary. I watched two women struggling to cross the line. Their legs had completely given way. They did the last few miles on their hands and knees crying in agony, dragging themselves with sheer grit and determination to complete this extraordinary achievement. This was, however, in stark contrast to the winner. This guy crossed the line like he had barely broken a sweat. Most people compete in the Ironman to see if they can complete it; they are not trying to win. That made me contemplate how fit and determined that winner must have been. What else must he be capable of? Take a moment to imagine how it must feel to WIN a triathlon.

It wasn't long after that I saw a TV show called the *Great Sperm Race*,[1] which was all about, as you would imagine, the journey of the sperm on its way to fertilize the human egg. The trailer describes it as 'the story of human conception as it's never been told before. With 250 million competitors, it is the most extreme race on Earth and there can only be one winner.' This got me thinking. Without going into the extreme examples, needless to say that sperm's challenges make the Ironman competition look like a kindergarten assault course. It truly is an intense journey of great distance and challenging hostile terrain with 250 million competitors.

Imagine how proud you would be to be that winner. Imagine winning a triathlon of those proportions and being better than a quarter of a billion other racers. That would be an achievement of a lifetime. Imagine what kind of a determined character you would need to be? What else might you be capable of? Well congratulations! That is exactly who you are. Even if you are young enough to have been mixed by hand in a test tube, or what my friend Piers calls 'a womb with a view,' you were still accepted by the egg in a job interview where you were up against hundreds of thousands of other candidates. Well done, you got the job.

At the point of conception, we have already achieved something extraordinary – top of an immensely large and competitive class. It is not surprising that we are so ready to bare our teeth and push and shove. You only need to close your eyes for a moment to feel the dynamic driving life force coursing through every fiber of your body, eager to survive and thrive. We are the offspring of that energy – that fight for life. You are already the winner of the most extraordinary race. Ideally we should all relax now but that kind of a thirst for life, or rather fight for life, doesn't subside easily. It is interesting to note that we call ourselves the human RACE. No wonder so many people are in such a hurry.

There were once laidback cavemen and women. They weren't too worried about storing food for winter or collecting enough firewood. They weren't especially concerned about keeping an eye out for saber-toothed tigers. They were confident, relaxed, and within a short while ... dead. They didn't survive and very few of their offspring survived either. We are not descended from them. We descended from the anxious ancestor. The over-cautious, nervous, and more fearful cave people. They survived. They ran faster, fought harder, and probably worried a lot. The anxious ancestors are our forefathers and if they could see how cushy our lives are in comparison they would be shellshocked that we spend time worrying about anything anymore.

Not only have we made it through the most extreme three-day fertility race, pitted against many millions of competitors, we have also made it through the historic ages. We have overcome the scavenging in the icy cold that was our harsh existence thousands of years ago. We have truly made it. We should be thrilled, but once again the abilities and feelings that enabled us to survive are still very much on automatic. This is a source of a lot of fear and resistance that unnecessarily puts us at odds with the world. Our ancestors would weep if they could see how ungrateful so many of us are. 'What,' they would ask, 'are you complaining about?'

THE BIG BEGINNING: THE WOMB AND BIRTH

For some people, their womb and birth experience can totally affect the way they see the world as an adult. When I first heard that these early experiences could affect our relationship to life, I scoffed at the ridiculousness of the idea. However, in my practice, I see these situations appearing over and over again, and when the associated fears are felt and contextualized amazing things happen. We can't easily recall memories from when we are very young because at that stage we were preverbal. That is to say, we had no words upon which to hang the experience. Imagine trying to tell me about your last vacation if you couldn't use any nouns, verbs, or adjectives.

Language gives our memory the framework to store and recall experience. Our birth memories may not be stored in a place that serves easy recall or description, but such an extreme experience of change in our environment (from womb to world) is definitely registered in some parts of our emotional memory. The pain and suffering that this can cause can be felt across generations, because when those fears are unresolved they can lead to all sorts of cripplingly negative feelings about our self and life.

BIRTH TRAUMA

Geraldine presented with a lack of confidence compounded by irreconcilable grief due to a series of miscarriages, which didn't appear to have a medical cause. The final one, ten years earlier, nearly killed her. She miscarried baby twins at seven months and to save her life the doctors had to perform a hysterectomy. When I started using the FreeMind techniques to help her journey into the feelings, it became clear that she had never forgiven herself. Deep down she felt that she had murdered her unborn children. Going deeper into her feelings about birth, life, and death, she started to access her own birth experience, describing being in a dangerous, dark, wet place, and became very anxious, claustrophobic, panicky, and uncomfortable.

Using the FreeMind techniques, I enabled her to stay present to the feelings so that she could work out what was going on. As we continued, it became clear that she was releasing the trauma that she had experienced during her own birth. She later told me that she was two weeks overdue and the doctors had used forceps to forcibly pull her out. When she was born her head was misshapen from the assisted birth and she was in a lot of pain. She had nearly died. Her underlying feeling of 'something being wrong,' which had undoubtedly affected her confidence all of her life, was due to her traumatic birth experience.

As we continued, it became clear to her that her inner mind and body had learned that staying in the womb a long time is 'bad.' Here, then, was an explanation for why she had had so many miscarriages. She had been trying to protect her children from a difficult birth out of love, so they wouldn't experience pain and discomfort. Her grief enabled her to access her early birth trauma, which meant she could once and for all let go of the idea that something was wrong with her and the sense that life is full of danger and threat. In many ways, losing her twins had now saved her.

In this one session, her grief disappeared. She finally understood why her body had done what it had done. Yes, it was afraid and overcautious and caused her terrible loss and grief, but had done so with the best of intentions. She was finally able to forgive herself. After the session she also reported feeling much more relaxed and confident about herself and life in general. She felt deeply grateful to her twins for being 'two perfect angels who were sent to save her.' It all made sense to her. It was perfect. Nothing was wrong. Peace prevailed.

....

Geraldine's experience is an extreme example but highlights the degree to which our birth can affect how we feel about life and ourselves in general. Sometimes having a beautiful womb experience can cause difficulties for us as adults too. Many people are driven to find their way back to the womb – back to that place of tranquility and calm. Back to that place where everything was taken care of, where there was nothing to be done. In many ways, that is our first imprint of unconditional love and deep inside us we hanker for relationships (and sometimes even jobs) that meet our every need without us having to do anything. This can sometimes result in us setting the bar so high that everything else falls short. We may even find ourselves stepping away from things that are actually good because of some impossible fantasy of something more perfect.

In my experience, this can prevent some people from being able to truly commit in relationships. Those people are with you but they also have one eye on who has just walked into the room. They might find it difficult to fully give themselves to anyone, so things don't work properly and they move from one relationship to another never feeling fully satisfied, continually searching for that 'perfect' love 'out there.' This is because the womb is the source of many fantasies that mean we say 'NO' to something that could actually have led to a life filled with many really wonderful YES moments. The key is building a relationship with yourself and life based on unconditional love. From there, we feel deeply connected with everything and everyone. The world becomes our loving womb in which we grow and develop. We feel part of something bigger, we feel provided for and loved, and we know deep down that everything is taken care of.

Returning to that state of saying 'YES' to life is a great surrender, a wonderful relaxant, and the foundation of all true and lasting happiness.

THE LOSS OF PARADISE: THE FIRST SIX MONTHS

When we are very young, we have no separate sense of self. We think of ourselves as everything else. There is no 'us' or 'other' to worry about. For a short while we are totally free. During the first six months, however, we begin to develop our separate sense of self. Early-years psychologists believe we become self-aware by eating. Supposedly, as food enters our body we start to get an idea of outside and inside, so becoming aware of ourselves and other things as separate objects. This can be a difficult time in our development, and can lead to being more prone to fear and resistance later on in life. In psychology this is called the 'primary wound' or the 'narcissistic wound.' This is where the personality or ego starts turning up to make sense of our world, to take control, and start creating a survival strategy. This fascinating concept is most easily explained by using an analogy from the Bible. So consider the following story not as a description of the beginning of mankind, but rather a beautiful description of what the early year psychologists have been discovering. Let us consider that this is the story of the beginning of all of us – the genesis of a typical human child.

Adam and Eve are in Eden, frolicking, free, naked, and blissfully happy with all their needs being met. The story then goes on to describe how Adam, having been given an apple by Eve, eats from the tree of self-knowledge and God becomes angry and throws them out of paradise. At our genesis, we are born into a paradise of no delineation, we have no separate sense of self, we are naked, free, beyond caring, and ideally (trauma and neglect aside) all our needs are met.

Then our mother (represented by Eve) gives us food, and this marks the beginning of our loss of Eden. The apple is a metaphor for the breast (similar looking too), and so as Adam (like all babies) eats he becomes self-aware as a distinct and separate individual. At that point in our early development, we begin to relate to ourselves as an object and realize that we are dependent on objects that are separate from us. This is a real and scary shock to the psychological system and that fear can lead us to question our safety. We realize we are not in control. We go from being free and happy without any self-consciousness to becoming little political beings trying to work out the best way to do things to get what we need.

It becomes clear to us as very young infants that there are some behaviors that are good and welcome (for example, cooing and laughing), and other behaviors that are bad and discouraged (for example, crying and throwing a tantrum). We don't have the wherewithal to understand the rules. This is scary. It also becomes clear to us that the people we are dependent on base their self-worth on the degree to which we validate them (for example, they look happy when we're laughing and scared or worried when we're crying). We begin to people-please and hide what we believe are our ugly truths. We do our best to cover up our fears and agendas, so that we can get what we want and need. That is when we lose our way. This is our loss of paradise. We look down on our helpless selves and feel exposed, less than, and dependent, so we hide our 'gross' and 'animal' nature by reaching for the fig leaf to cover ourselves and lose everything.

The development from infant to young person is fraught with pretense, posturing, and posing, and this blocks the authentic self-expression that underpins all happiness. We edit ourselves to fit what we believe is required. The fig leaf in Eden is a metaphor that represents our personality. The root word of personality is 'persona,' which is the Latin word for 'mask.' Our personality sets about representing what we want the world to see. We start to hide our truth and, in that very act, lose our way. Those early decisions can go on to affect who we are and how we turn up in the world as adults. The ancient Taoist Chinese master Lao-Tzu dedicated most of his writings to the concept of natural balance and the order that occurs when things are left in their natural state. He said,

> *'When heaven is on earth, wild horses fertilize the fields. When heaven is not on earth war horses are bred at the frontier.'*
>
> Lao-Tzu

Our Eden, our heaven on Earth, our place of peace exists inside us as strongly as it ever did. When we transcend our perception of ourselves as separate we relax into the flow of life and things naturally work out for the best. The reality of who we really are is a wondrous interconnected field of conscious energy. Leaving aside the scientific discoveries that prove this, which we'll discuss later (see pages 184–8), we can experience the vast beauty and love of that interconnectedness field at any moment. There is nothing stopping you right now from putting this book down and breathing deeply into yourself, letting out three deep breaths and experiencing yourself (ourself really) as part of a single field of consciousness. That is the truth of who you are and spirituality is just whatever practice you use to remember that unity.

The journey from infancy starts with the undifferentiated amorphous experience of the pre-personal, which is essentially the deeply connected oneness experience but without any conscious awareness of it. We then move into the personal stage of identification of ourselves as a separate being, where we are dogged by fears of inadequacy, fear for our own survival, and resistance to the flow of life. The aim therefore of the three Pillars Practices (which you'll discover in Part II) is to help you move toward a transpersonal perception of yourself: not defined by the limited personality but rather by our limitless universality – from the pre-personal, to the personal, through to the transpersonal. This is the FreeMind Experience and it is the source of absolute happiness.

THE FALL FROM YES: 18 MONTHS TO THREE YEARS OLD

For the first 18 months of our life, we ideally live in a world of support, care, and attention. When we are hungry we are fed, when we are sleepy we are carried to bed, when we need changing we are given fresh clothes. Everything happens magically. Essentially we get what we want and things seem to be seamlessly organized around our needs. Then as soon as we can walk everything changes. Those people (our parents/caregivers) who seemed to be there to help us now seem to be there to get in our way and thwart our desires, telling us 'Put that down,' 'Don't touch that,' 'Don't climb that,' 'No, stop it, not there, not now, not that way ...' and so on.

This is a confusing time. What have we done that is so terrible? Why has everything changed? Why are these people stopping us and getting in our way? What mistake have we made? What message have we missed? What is it all about? Why are we feeling so squashed, put upon, restricted, blocked, and told off? This is a boiling mixture of anguish, frustration, and terror. Something significant has changed and we don't know why. We are not able to get everything we want, and are dependent on these other people with whom we cannot properly communicate, and who seem to be inconsistent in their willingness to give us what we want.

At exactly that same time, our awareness that these people are dependent on us to feel good about themselves deepens. We sense accurately that our mood affects them. We have the power to upset them and the power to make them happy. On one level, this feels good, but on another level it is wholly unsettling. We don't want to be able to have the power to have such an influence on the people around us. We don't want their happiness and contentment to have anything to do with who we are.

I notice this with my daughter. I notice how parts of me really want to modify her mood at times. I notice how at times I put pressure on her to not be emotional. I try to get her to be rational. This is not my parenting plan. I just catch myself doing it. At times, I notice that I try to manipulate and steer her by letting her know that when she is 'good' I am happy. And by good I mean happy, well behaved, and willing to do what I want. This seems like fairly normal parenting on one level but it carries with it a number of dangerous messages that can actually unsettle children's young minds, making them much less secure.

Children don't want their anger or difficulties to frustrate/scare us. How scary for a child to feel that his or her parents' level of security is based on how they are behaving. Yet, most children pick this stuff up very early on. I first noticed this with my daughter when I realized that sometimes she was laughing at my jokes and my games to make me feel good about myself. She was already a political being playing a game of 'feel good.'

HONORING YOUR CHILD'S FEELINGS

One day when my daughter was two, she was in a difficult mood all day but it peaked with what seemed to be a totally unreasonable tantrum. Desperate for her to be more reasonable or logical, I fell to my knees and shouted at her. I felt terrible afterwards but it didn't help. She cried intensely for a while and then just lay face down on the carpet, seemingly crestfallen and depressed. She had never done this before. I could tell she wasn't sulking because there was no anger in what she was doing. No, this was flat, despondent and deflated, and I found it unbearable. I guessed I must have really scared her – and, worse, disappointed her. Anyway I resisted all urges to go and cheer her up. This time, instead of trying to change her, I let her have her feelings.

Later on, we had some food and did our usual bath-bedtime routine and she was happy again. Wrapped in a towel, she was bristling with fun and joy and my heart broke wide open. I was mesmerized by the love I felt for her, and in an incredibly present and powerful way I became very still and we made beautiful eye contact. She stopped wriggling and became totally still (which is unusual for her), and I simply, but congruently, told her that I loved her. I tell her this many times a day but this time she really seemed to feel the wave of love that the words were carried upon. She paused and tentatively said, 'Sometimes I cry?' That was all she said, but with that she seemed to be checking in with me. It really felt like she was asking me. 'Do you still love me when I cry?'

My behavior had meant she was worrying that I loved or liked her less. She really didn't know and it was scary for her. I scooped her up and I told her I loved her all the time, no matter what she did, I told her I love her when she is happy, I told her I love her when she is sad, when she is angry, and so on. We laughed and giggled together but I still felt awful. Later, when I was reading her a story, she stopped me, made eye contact and said, 'Daddy good,' and then put her head back on my chest. She had forgiven me, and so I finished reading with tears streaming down my face. I walked out of her room marveling at how much I had to learn and feeling deeply honored that I had this incredible little being in my life who could show me the way.

....

Many of us learned as children that our impassioned and angry outbursts were 'too much' for our parents. When we were difficult, not ideal, less than perfect, it was annoying, had to be stopped, had to be different, had to be good, better when quiet, much better when happy, naughty when sad, less fun when difficult. What dark times those must have been when we, in our beds and cots, went to sleep worrying about who we were, how we must be different, and what we must do to win back the lost love of our parents. People talk about the terrible twos because many children become difficult at that age. Is it the children who are really difficult? What markers are we using to assess 'good'? What if we allowed our children their moods? What if we allowed their emotions? What if we could hold a space for them where we didn't make them feel that our own self-worth was somehow dependent on them behaving in a certain kind of way?

More often than not, our ability as parents to hold steady while our children are being emotional is directly proportional to the extent to which we are comfortable with our own emotional upsets. Heavily repressed parents make for heavily repressed children. Parents that operate with Emotional Intelligence are much more able to help their children understand and manage their emotions. You might want to spend some time considering your childhood years. Ask yourself the following questions:

* How open were your parents?
* Were difficult things talked about openly in your home?
* Were negative emotions ignored and brushed under the carpet?
* Were there high levels of conflict?
* Did your family members take responsibility for their own feelings or did they blame other people for how they were feeling?
* To what degree were your parents or caregivers able to stay present with you while you struggled?
* What are your beliefs about anger and emotion?
* Did you have to be a good little boy or a nice girl?
* How might 'trying to be good' have affected you and your relationship with yourself?
* How might that mean that your life is not a totally accurate reflection of who you really are?

When all of us is loved and accepted fully – including all our rage, despair, rebelliousness, and naughtiness – we are much more likely to believe and trust in ourselves. We are much more likely to grow up to be ourselves. The FreeMind Experience is essentially a re-parenting process where we get to meet every aspect of ourselves with love. This is the bedrock of all true self-expression, all confidence and lasting success – this is the foundation for absolute happiness.

THE PECKING ORDER: THE SIBLING LOTTO

The order of your birth can play a huge part in your conditioning too. No two families are the same and every family order will have a different effect. At the same time there are some factors worth being aware of. This is especially true if the second child arrives when the first child is between 18 months and three years old. At that stage they are already questioning the degree to which they are loved by their parents. The first child can already be struggling with understanding what they have done to fall from grace so profoundly. Then along comes another child. Not surprisingly, it is very common for firstborns to imagine that the second child has come along as a result of them being faulty or not good enough. They are already worrying about why their world is now more NO than YES, and then a second child comes along and gets all of the attention. This can make the firstborn feel 'less than' or, worse, they can feel as if they have been replaced.

The brilliant animated film *Toy Story* tells the story of the dearly loved cowboy toy called Woody being replaced in his young owner's affections by a new toy, Buzz Lightyear. Everyone makes a fuss over Buzz but Woody knows he is silly and ridiculous. No wonder the movie was such a success as it exposes the pain of the firstborn being usurped by a second child. The follow-up movies show the two characters coming to terms with each other and becoming good brotherly friends. If you watch the movie for that symbolism alone, you realize just how cleverly and accurately it portrays this common human experience.

In my practice, I have noticed a tendency, although not universally true, for firstborns to suffer from a ghostly sense that something is wrong with them. This fear expands into their general consciousness, and starts expressing itself as a genuine concern that something is truly physically wrong with them. The majority of (but not all) hypochondriacs I have treated were firstborns. However, the impact of feeling 'less than' doesn't always have a detrimental long-term effect on a person's place in the world. Many of the world's highest achievers are firstborns. Many are compelled to battle against their sense of being 'less than.' They work harder and push themselves to overcome their fear of not being good enough. This can lead to greatness.

In contrast, it is also common for second-born children not to apply themselves as hard, not because they are less academic but because the 'high achiever' role has already been taken in the family. So, instead of competing directly, they maybe decide to be the sporty one, or the more social one. It makes sense that many of these early identities and personality traits are formed as attempts to make the family dynamic work. These arbitrary roles are confirmed and encouraged by parents – who are often more comfortable with their children in different categories too. This is less about the truth of our natural personality and much more about fear and control. Unfortunately these ways of being (personality categories/styles) can become so familiar that we grow up sincerely believing that is who we are.

BIRTH ORDER

I was the second-born child in my family and my arrival was very bad news for my brother. A power struggle developed between us, and I grew up feeling very confused about him. I certainly felt that he hated me. The underlying sensation I experienced was a very real sense that I ruined his life and, for a long time, I think I probably did. Our family was a warzone of bickering, which must have been horrific for our parents. Now having my own child, I can only imagine how heartbreaking it must be to have the two people you love the most in the world seemingly hating each other. I now realize that I didn't hate him at all. It was just more comfortable to hate him than it was to feel his constant rejection of me. I knew my presence was a disturbance to him and for many years, me being myself seemed to intrinsically annoy my brother. This unsettled him, which unsettled my mother and from very early on in life I linked 'being myself' with all sorts of bad things.

When going through the layers of these defenses, I found a little brother heart that wanted a loving big brother. I defended against these vulnerable and rejected feelings by being remote, competitive, arrogant, condescending, and all manner of other ways of being that were distant and negative. This prevented my brother and I from being as close as I would have liked. In turn, my coping strategies kept my brother at a distance but they also affected how I turned up in the world. I was ready to be isolated, less willing to be included, more likely to go my own way, and struggled with believing that it was OK to be fully myself. This had a huge impact on the choices I made and the degree to which I allowed myself to put myself out there and try.

Challenging family dynamics and the ensuing NO moments lead us to compensate or manage the perceived 'problem,' and so live in ways that aren't the fullest expression of our greatest possibility. If you have siblings then it might be worthwhile spending some time thinking about the following questions:

* How might your birth order be affecting you?
* What roles have you and your siblings taken on that don't fully reflect who you are?
* How would it feel to take on another role?
* How receptive would your family be to seeing you in another light, and how long would it take them?

Imagine for a moment that many of your choices about your interests (and possibly the subjects you chose to study) were more about creating comfortable roles in the family than they were about your true preferences.

* How might you have chosen differently if you had been the eldest, middle, or youngest sibling?
* What were the unspoken rules about achieving in your family?

The human mind is so strong and yet so frail. Fragments of fear coagulate into half-baked ideas that grasp but a fraction of the actual truth. Those conglomerations form a filter through which we see the world and they create a foundation upon which our self-value rests. That process is the forming of our personality. It is not actually who we are. It is who we have become and we can revisit these ideas; and we can release these feelings and change how our past affects us today. We can't change what happened in our past but what happened isn't actually that important. It is what we make our past mean. That is the only thing that counts and that can be changed.

THE FIRST SHOCK OF OUR OWN DARKNESS

When we are young, we are on many levels selfish little beasts. As adults we understand this about children and do our best to civilize them, ideally without crushing their spirits too much. Unfortunately we don't have that awareness when we are younger. At some point we come face to face with our dark side and without any compassionate context it can be pretty disturbing to find out that in some ways we are not actually, always that nice.

SEEING MY DARK SIDE

When I was seven, we used to have sport on Wednesday afternoon. When we were freed from class, it was always a race to see who could get to the changing rooms first, and on that day I definitely wanted to be quickest.

Actually, as I am writing this, I am listening to *Caliban's Dream*, famously played at the 2012 London Olympics opening ceremony; the track is full of optimism and drive, so it's the perfect accompaniment for the recounting of this memory. Imagine me with an uplifting soundtrack, in the lead running as fast as I can with the clatter of my competitors close on my tail, but my eye was on the prize – my heart full of drive. My legs moving like pistons, I can hear Ralph Mayer a few steps behind me. I get my hand on the door of the changing room and in moments I am in, and am fully triumphant. To make sure everyone reveres my greatness, I slam the door behind me. Had it shut fully it would have done so with an almighty bang, but unfortunately (music screeches to a stop) the door slams with full force into Ralph – and being only seven, his head is perfectly level with the door handle, which he runs into at full tilt and his eyebrow promptly explodes with blood.

I had done a bad thing – a very bad thing. I had been trying to do a good thing. However, the obvious darkness of my competitiveness wasn't the only problem. That was bad enough but something worse was going on in my head. What introduced me most clearly to a more shocking level of my darkness was that my first wave of concern was not for Ralph and his eye. It was for me. I *knew* I had done something wrong and I could see and certainly hear that Ralph was in a lot of pain. The blood alone was disturbing but what was infinitely more disturbing was the fact that I was more worried about the trouble that I might be in. It was like finding an 'inner beastie' I didn't know was there until that point. I didn't like that discovery. I did feel bad for Ralph but I knew my order of concerns wasn't the 'right' way around. I felt I had happened upon something very ugly deep inside. This was sad news that I quickly brushed away. I wish I had been prepared better for that moment.

· ·

You, me, and everyone has a dark side or energy – it is a natural part of our being. Because I wish I had understood this as a child, I have been teaching my daughter about her inner beastie, so that she can understand her dark side in a more loving way. To do this, I have simply been drawing her attention to that part of herself when it comes out. For example, when she wants to playfight. I help her understand that aggression and competitiveness is normal. So, when I see that facet of her rise, I get her to embody it totally. We both attack cushions and prowl and growl like wild animals. This usually ends up with us rolling around giggling and feeling much lighter.

Knowing the truth of our warrior energy lets us choose to stay on the useful side of it. The denial of it, gives it power. After hurting Ralph Mayer, I didn't dwell on being that awful person. I hid it away from myself and did my best to hope that no one would notice it. I was revolted by myself and therefore scared of what I might, one day, do. Another time, I remember playing with a friend's toy and mistakenly pulling it apart. I hastily looked over my shoulder and surreptitiously propped the toy up on a shelf so that it wouldn't be discovered until someone else played with it. That all added to my fears about my inherent 'badness.'

When our dark side is known and expressed then it enables us to feel much better, so you might want to spend some time thinking about your inner beastie, and ask yourself the following questions:

* Do you remember times when your competitiveness or self-centeredness led you to behave in ways that hurt others?

* Do you remember worrying about being found out for something, supposedly, 'terrible' that you did?
* How did you feel when you were discovered or hid that part of yourself away?
* Where are you at with your dark side/energy?
* Are you in touch with your inner warrior?

It is the things we tell ourselves and the fears we hide from ourselves in these moments that can go on to hold us back later on in life. These unresolved moments can lead to us not fully trusting ourselves. These NO-to-us moments can stop us from being able to truly love ourselves. In turn, this can stop us from ever truly relaxing and can make the idea of being deeply intimate with another person very scary. Full acceptance of self is the only thing that makes real intimacy possible. Real intimacy with ourselves is the only thing that makes happiness possible.

Being at peace with my aggressive warrior energy, I recognize, understand, and support that part of myself to help it find better ways to express its competitive and protective energies. Many men feel that there is so much pressure on them to be 'nice' sensitive guys that they feel ashamed of their aggressive masculine energy. Men not in touch with their feelings are not always dysfunctional. It is sometimes part of what actually enables them to function in a challenging or dangerous situation. Women, of course, have their own beautiful warrior energy too. To get a hint of that, criticize a mother's child and you will see a flash of anger a lioness would be proud of.

Anger and rage and our capacity to destroy are not intrinsically bad. We have in those core primal energies parts of ourselves that would do extraordinarily heroic things in times of great need. To deny that and think of ourselves as wholly nice involves a disconnection from a place that is actually a source of some of our greatest passions. These early perceptions of our primal protective and competitive energies can have a huge impact on how we let ourselves be fully expressive when we are older. The full FreeMind Experience involves putting your loving arms around every aspect of your being. Finding those early moments, where we panicked about how nice and good we were, and letting every part of us know that all parts are welcome. All parts are loved. All parts are included, valued, and needed within the whole. This creates the possibility for you to live as a fully expressed, lively, vibrant, powerful, and fully sexual being.

THE FIRST QUESTIONING OF OUR PARENTS: THE LOVE TEMPLATE

Up until the age of about six or seven, we believe all parents are like our parents. It is only when we get a little older and start visiting our friends' families that we begin to understand that not all parents are created equal. At that point, we can't help but realize that our parents are individuals in their own right. We then begin to assess them in ways that we never have before. This is a mixed bag. Usually, we will try to defend ourselves against any negative realizations we might have and it is those defense mechanisms that can go on to cause all sorts of difficulties for us.

Realizing that our parents aren't perfect can be very scary. Realizing that some people don't like our parents can also be disturbing, as can the realization that sometimes we don't like them either. More commonly we get a sense that they are afraid, in need of our validation, they don't have all the answers, they are struggling with life, don't enjoy work, don't love each other, and so on. This can start to lay down fearful patterns regarding what we think about life. The bursting of this idealization bubble can hugely affect the model of the world that we then begin to work with or against.

Our early judgments about our parents are usually projected onto the world. So, in practical terms, that means if our parents have affairs and struggle in love, we tend to think that is what love and life is like. In contrast, the people whose parents have a good and lasting relationship are much more likely to believe in love. The FreeMind approach involves helping people remove the conditioned filters through which they see the world, getting beyond the expectations that are laid down by what we have seen and experienced as we were growing up. Freeing our minds of these often limiting beliefs is the key to bringing your best to life, so you might want to ask yourself the following questions:

* What are your beliefs about love?
* Did your parents' relationship inspire you?
* Did they make love look good?
* Did your parents openly show love toward each other?
* What was the family culture/story about work, money, and success?
* What was the family culture/story about education?
* What was the family culture/story about class or their place in the social structure?

* How was your family around food and exercise?

Understanding how your family's culture affects your perspective can be hugely liberating. In that process we can begin to free our minds of all sorts of limiting conditioning. That allows us to build lives that are a true reflection of who we really are.

A WORLD OF COMPETITION AND COMPARISON

With the very best of intentions most parents want their children to do well. They want them to develop rapidly and learn all the information, skills, and attitudes that they think their children need to do well in the world. This is all done to help the child thrive. While all that is admirable, it can also go on to be part of why so many adults don't feel good about themselves. It can deeply confirm a child's sense that where you are 'now' is not OK. Being 'OK' is all about getting 'over there.' You must walk, you must talk, you must use the bathroom, and you must work hard, sit still, and do well at school.

When they start school, most children quickly realize that most educational establishments are built on the same 'not OK yet' principles. Everything is about competition and getting somewhere else. So it's not surprising, that 14 or so years later, the beautiful, playful, and naturally happy child is anxious, competitive, afraid, stressed, and filled with all sorts of deeply held beliefs that they are not good enough.

Whenever there is competition there is, of course,

comparison. When we look to other people to see how we are doing, we are lost. There are always those that are better or worse than us. This leads to vanity or fear, but far worse than that, it programs us to define ourselves externally. This is one of the core drivers of materialism that prevents us from being happy. Children need to be taught about self-discipline and they need to be encouraged to apply themselves, but more than anything they need their core validity confirmed internally. In other words, people need to be taught how to feel good about themselves because of what they think, not because of what someone else thinks or how they compare to others. With that, everything else falls into place. Without that, people grow up struggling against all sorts of unnecessary limiting beliefs and feelings.

....

THE DANGER OF COMPARISON

Being the third son of a very competitive and academic family, Bernard was expected to follow in the footsteps of his two elder brothers, both high achievers, and fulfill his parents' incredibly high expectations. This young man was, however, not gifted academically. He had his own intelligence and was incredibly funny. He had a real way about himself that people loved. He was handsome and incredibly popular, and yet remained kind-hearted and considerate. He was one of those standout people that you knew was going to go a long way. He was destined to be a fantastic entertainer.

When he took his exams at 18, he attained excellent passes but his grades weren't as high as his brothers'. Unable to bear the shame of comparison to his brothers, he committed suicide. What a dark day that must have been for his parents. What a terrible shock and an awful wake-up call to the things that are actually important in life.

. . . .

Fortunately, Bernard's story is an exceptional one but it clearly demonstrates how our parents' demands can affect and damage us. Yes, it makes sense for parents to do their best to inspire their children to make the most of themselves. However, unless it is balanced with unconditional love, which lets us believe that we are perfect as we are, we may end up feeling 'not good enough' or having failed. Take a moment to consider how much of your early years were about competition, comparison, and pressure to improve. League tables, bell-curve grading, school races, the first dating and kissing conquests, big breasts or no breasts yet, boys begging their voices and their balls to drop, competing against other schools, other teams, the national average, being in or out, the cool kid or the dropout and everything else in between. Just thinking about it is exhausting but how has it affected you?

* Did you give up?
* Did you get addicted to proving the world wrong?
* Did you go your own way?
* Were you listening to the beat of another drummer or were you just too afraid to dance with the others?

Understanding how you responded in those moments is an important part of becoming free. Many of us choose to engage in life in certain ways in response to competition and comparison. That isn't always a real reflection of who you really are or who you might have been had those pressures not been there. Take a moment to consider how much easier and happier life might have been without competition and comparison. Maybe it drove you forward and helped you achieve great things but at the same time it may have undermined how good you feel about yourself in general.

DISAPPOINTING FRIENDS

When we are younger, the first time one of our friends lets us down can be incredibly disturbing. These disappointments can create some very painful ideas and limiting beliefs about loyalty and relationships, which can go on to shape how we function, trust, and love as adults. In truth, there is evidence everywhere of extraordinary human generosity and many people would say that their friendships have been a constant source of inspiration for them. Sometimes in times of trouble it is incredible to see who will drop everything to be at our side when we need a friend more than anything. However, there are disappointing times when we are growing up that can hugely affect our ability to believe in other people.

PLAYGROUND BETRAYAL

In the school playground, I experienced my first major disappointment in a friend. I was ten and had a huge crush on one of my classmates, Joanne. I had barely spoken to her, but I watched her a lot as she played with her friends. She struck me as being really confident, so I decided I was going to ask her to be my girlfriend at lunchtime. That morning I didn't concentrate much in lessons. I was too busy wistfully imagining walking round the athletics track holding hands with Joanne. When the bell rang for 10.30am break, I was already nervous but also very excited. So excited in fact, I proudly told Paul, one of my closest friends, my plans.

Paul listened intently, as a good friend should, and just as I had finished Joanne came into view, walking across the playground with two of her friends. Here was my girlfriend-to-be – how exciting. At that moment, Paul sprung to his feet and in an instant I could see he was up to something. He looked at me and laughed. I could see the spite in his eyes, and braced myself for what I thought would be an incredibly embarrassing exposure. I was sure he was going to blurt out my plans and mock me horribly.

Unfortunately it was much worse than that. He bowled straight up to her and said, 'Do you want to be my girlfriend?' She looked thrilled and agreed immediately. I was absolutely gutted. I had seen how much he enjoyed taking her away from me. I realized at that point that he was not my friend. Or worse, that he was my friend, but that didn't mean much. This had a profound impact on me. It was a very real disappointment that led me for many years to be very cautious about sharing certain things with male friends.[2]

....

Most of us have had those moments when we realized that some of our early friendships didn't run that deep; times also when we realized that when it actually mattered some of our adult friendships didn't count for much either. Too many friendships fall down when honoring that friendship involves inconvenience to the other party. Those disappointments can putrefy our belief system and really affect the degree to which we let people in when we are older. Take some time to revisit these NO memories to ensure that they are not dangerously skewing your perception.

Such disappointments can prevent us from remembering those golden characters who can be relied upon – who will still be there for us, even when it is inconvenient or, even better, when we are so off our path that we are lost, broken, destructive, or disgusting. Some of my darkest moments have been utterly saved by those few friends who, despite my worst being fully on show, didn't shy away from me. If anything they have run all the faster to catch me. Take a moment to consider those moments in your life when a friend was really there for you. Making a practice of remembering the acts of selfless service that blow your heart wide open is an essential antidote to the accumulation of disappointments that can otherwise distort your happiness.

Underneath all of the fear and resistance, competition, and aggression, the human heart and its capacity to love is truly the greatest natural wonder of the world.

THE SURPRISE OF THE 'REAL' WORLD

When we are children, we generally hope (and expect) that the adult world is one of integrity and inspiration. To our dismay, as we get older, we discover quite rapidly that the 'real' world is fraught with moral degradation and complication. Our parents lose their godlike powers, politicians lie and embezzle, marketers manipulate, businesses exploit, bad music is more popular than good music, bad art is more popular than good art, the church oppresses, wars are waged, people in power abuse, victims attract further victimization, and the gap between the 'haves' and the 'have nots' is widening all of the time. All of these disappointments (NO feelings) can heavily blind us to the beauty of the human spirit and to the wondrousness of life.

All of the world's struggles are held in place by the principles of materialism, which drive our craving for security, wealth, and power. This is owing to our unresolved fears and resistance to life, but it creates a commercial world where our Western society's values appear, in many ways, to be somewhat crooked. Becoming aware of this fact as we grow into young adults is disappointing. How we deal with that frustration goes on to affect how we engage in the world. However, at a deeper level, living in this type of society means we are also bombarded with messages every day that confirm the very kind of thinking that makes it harder for us to be happy.

In particular, the advertising and the marketing industries confirm and sustain much of the kind of thinking that causes much of the unhappiness in the world. It affirms the idea that something 'external' to you is the solution to your unhappiness. The main sticking pain of the ego structure is its addiction to this idea that someone or something will solve the problem of 'you.' Will bring the final peace, will secure the future, and will save the day. More money, more freedom, more houses, a pair of shoes for every occasion, the perfect stereo, the fastest car, the flawless spiritual teacher, the most powerful drug, the best medical care, more time with your beloved, less time with annoying forms, fewer plans and more action – the mind thriving on the idea that when things are different 'out there,' things will be different in ourselves. Many of our social institutions and common (manipulative) commercial practices make living in harmony and happiness so much harder.

Take some time to think about the things you 'want' and consider how the process of 'wanting' brings more stress and anxiety to your life. The FreeMind Practices in Part II are all about finding that center point of wholeness and completeness. That place in you that knows your happiness and contentment is all to do with your relationship with yourself. From that place of real inner peace and power all external addictions and insatiable cravings dissolve away.

Freeing the mind of these limiting and happiness-destroying beliefs is a vital part of bringing our lives back into balance.

THE FEAR OF DEATH

The ultimate NO that underpins so many of our other NOs comes from our resistance to death. So much of my clinical work is about helping people to realize that they are actually pretty upset about the fact that they, and everyone they love, are going to die. It is very often this unresolved frustration that becomes the filter through which we see all other frustrations and find them impossible. Our relationship to that knowledge can totally determine how willing we are to engage in life and love.

This upset underlies many people's dysfunctional relationship to life. Some people lie and manipulate, others try and do the minimum or overwork to get enough money to buy freedom, or beat the system. Some want to go off-grid. Others project their upset about death onto the world and it turns into a deeply resistant cynicism and pessimism about the world. Other people dedicate their lives to being activists, to fixing the problem 'out there,' without realizing they are really battling against their fear of death. If we are against death, we are set against life. Underneath it all, we have an inability to accept the natural flow and cycle of life. This hugely affects our ability to relax; it blocks our natural enjoyment and very often makes it impossible for us ever to be truly still. This prevents us from ever being truly present and that cuts us off from the richest source of happiness possible. All of the greatest magic occurs when we are fully present to the moment in its entirety.

When we are terrified of death we live in opposition to life, trying to cheat the system and find some way to live forever. This is the manic stage of the bipolar crescendo – the frenzied, frenetic, expansive megalomania that believes it will be quick enough, rich enough, smart enough, artistic enough, or attractive enough to live forever. Or we will make such a difference to the world that our mark will be there to be seen for millennia after we've gone. But then we crash and our relentless mortality like an inescapable cloud overshadows everything and strips the joy from our greatest achievements. Nothing feels quite as good as we hoped. None of the 'stuff' fills the gap. There is no real satisfaction in anything and we are haunted by a hollowness that gnaws coldly at our connection to the meaning of life.

From the perspective of the small, limited, fearful, and disconnected personality, there is no escape from death and therefore no point to anything and no real happiness is possible. The FreeMind Experience is all about connecting more deeply to your eternal, universal nature beyond the fear and identification of the limited and separate personality.

Overcoming these fears, and the resultant compensatory beliefs and behaviors, is really the ultimate way to enjoy life.

One of the things I like to do with large groups is to help people protect their happiness from future upsets. This might sound a little strange but it's guaranteed that we will all lose people that we love at some point in our lives. When that happens it can be difficult not to let it affect our faith in life. We can become overwhelmed with a sense of pointlessness and hopelessness. So, this process can help us to prepare for the event by giving the universe consent for our loved ones to die. I know it sounds morbid but it actually leads to a much deeper appreciation of them.

This process is all about learning to let go before life gets difficult. This means that when the inevitable happens, you are already much more prepared for it but it also means you are much more likely to make the most of your loved ones now. We don't often treat people as though they won't always be around but that is, of course, the truth. If you want to try this for yourself, ask yourself the following questions and take the appropriate action:

* Are you complete with everyone in your life?
* Is there anything that you would like to say to someone that you care about deeply? Why wait? How could you cherish your loved ones now?
* Have you expressed love to all your relatives?
* Have you told your parents that you love them?
* Have you asked them to tell you that they love you?
* Is there someone that you would love to ask for a hug or more?
* Are you totally clear about where your grandparents lived?
* Do you have your family's full story?
* Would it be worth interviewing your relatives about their lives and capturing it on video, so that the future generations may have something to know them by and the family stories can be preserved? Let's bring back the ancient oral traditions and capture them with modern technology.

Our resistant relationship to death often means we don't think long and hard about the many things that we could do to be much better prepared for our death and the deaths of our loved ones. Doing this kind of preparation future-proofs your faith and your happiness. Of course, it doesn't mean you won't be grief stricken if they become ill or die, but you will have made the most of loving and cherishing them while they were alive. It is wise to make the most of your precious time by accepting every aspect of life and death, embracing it all so that you are in the best frame of mind to make the most of this wonderful life.

The Triple YES of FreeMind is the total unconditional and loving acceptance of everything, including death. This is the foundation of absolute happiness.

CHAPTER 4

Balancing the Three Pillars

Part II presents the Three FreeMind Pillars and Practices. I am certain that if you apply them to your life, you will experience much more success and happiness. The FreeMind Practices are incredibly effective but it is very important that you keep all three practices in balance. Emotional Intelligence, Success Psychology, and Oneness Philosophy are incredible tools but without balance they can be dangerous. I say this from personal experience because, a few years ago, I totally lost my way. I share some more of that story with you now, so that you can avoid making the same mistakes that I made.

A FALL FROM GRACE

By 2005 I had been working with clients for five years and my motivation began to change. As my work evolved, I started to get really interested in spreading the word about Emotional Intelligence, Success Psychology, and Oneness Philosophy. I began to see more clearly than ever that if everyone learned these techniques, the world would become a much more beautiful place. At the same time, I was also getting very excited because the work I was doing with music and hypnotherapy was proving to be extremely successful in helping people to heal rapidly. However, I was still using other people's music and didn't have the full capacity to create the exact musical journeys for my clients that I wanted.

That situation changed in 2006 when I started working with Mike Trim, a brilliant composer of music for films. Together we created a range of therapeutic and inspirational soundtracks, designed to take people on very specific musical metaphorical journeys. The combination of spoken word, hypnosis, motivational psychology, and inspirational music is very powerful. Using these bespoke soundtracks and guided visualizations, I found that anyone could learn all of the FreeMind techniques to make all of the changes they wanted without the need for an expensive therapist. I was absolutely convinced that this would solve the world's biggest problems, and therefore started promoting my 'cure-all' to everyone I could. I was passionate, but I had also become rigid and caught up with the idea that the world not being emotionally intelligent was the 'problem.' This was the beginning of my very slow, very painful fall from grace.

I borrowed a large sum of money to complete the FreeMind library of recordings and I was so sure it would be a winner that I started winding down my private practice. The problem was I was no longer a therapist; I was a social entrepreneur with something 'important' to do. I was trying to be everything to everyone. Some days I was going into big businesses as a corporate-change trainer.[3] Other days, I visited prisons to champion reducing reoffending rates; and also providing Emotional Intelligence training, which I'm still passionate about, to kids in schools.

In each situation, I was doing everything I could to make myself fit what I thought they wanted to hear. I was not truly myself anywhere. At the same time, I was so enamored with making therapy and the FreeMind Training affordable for everyone, I started feeling guilty about charging my clients. I saw unconditional love as the answer for everyone and couldn't reconcile that with charging money. So, I started offering my services on a donation-only basis and started helping as many people as I could.

It is a beautiful thing to see all things as perfect and to continuously respond to life in an open and loving way, but it is essential that we include within that our own needs and boundaries.

By 2008 nothing was working and I was burned out and exhausted. I wasn't bringing in any of the big organizational change contracts, I wasn't selling hundreds of hypnosis recordings, and my private practice was now making a fraction of what it did because I'd made it so easy for people not to pay me. I thought I was being beautiful (spiritually advanced) and trusted that I would be looked after. I now realize that I wasn't looking after myself. I wasn't including myself in my love. I continued like this for a further two years, meaning that by 2010 I had spent five years totally overextending myself and over giving, and didn't protect myself appropriately from other people's needs and dysfunctions.

All the while I kept telling myself that if I were more enlightened then I wouldn't mind. I kept just working on my side of the fence to manage my internal response to what was happening. I encouraged myself to meditate more, and to let it go more. I berated myself for being an egotist because surely only my ego was that part of me that cared about being treated nicely. If I could be happy no matter what, then I should surely be able to remain peaceful within the storm of another person's attack.

SPIRITUAL BYPASS

With hindsight, I realize that was all very admirable but it added up to being a total walkover. In the name of love, I had forgotten myself in the middle. This is spiritual bypass and it is one of the biggest dangers of any spiritual practice – where we use our spiritual practice and our newfound resilience as a way of avoiding uncomfortable thoughts, feelings, and facts. Using spiritual philosophy and practices in this way is just like reaching for a beer. Meditation can be totally abused as a tranquilizer. Always being 'nice' and accommodating is not the sign of enlightenment. The aggressive roar or attack of a lioness when protecting her cubs is as holy as any pacifist's fear-covering smile.

Spiritual bypass can prevent us from standing up for ourselves: Saying what needs to be said and doing what needs to be done. Enlightenment is not a passive relationship to life where we just accept everyone's treatment of us.

Sometimes we love 'what is' by honoring our honest (angry, hurt, defensive, aggressive, and so on) response to what is happening, and use the fire in our belly to motivate us to do something about it. Otherwise, spiritual practice runs the risk of becoming just another form of denial.

SPIRITUAL MATERIALISM

So, at that time, there were some key areas in my work and my relationships where I wasn't looking after myself. After five years of struggling, my life, my marriage, and my faith were in tatters. My magical relationship with this divine and perfect universe had fallen apart. Things no longer seemed blessed and perfect.

Not only was I in spiritual bypass but I was also trapped by spiritual materialism. This is where the idea that 'something external is the answer' creeps into our spiritual practice. We step away from having a shallow existence, where we just want more stuff and money, in order to become spiritual. We start going on courses, getting clean, living well and maybe doing yoga, meditation, or some other practice. We're no longer obsessed with owning a big house and a flash car but dream instead of doing a full headstand, meditating for hours on end, and 'getting to' enlightenment.

This is simply swapping one set of shallow material goals for a set of spiritual material goals. When spiritual materialism is at play it is very easy for us to be captured by the idea that there is right and wrong, there is somewhere to go, there is some 'thing' that will save the day that 'needs' to be 'made' to happen. In my case, that spiritual materialism peaked with my desire to save the world. I saw the world as something needing saving and I felt I was the one to do it.

SPIRITUAL ACTIVISM

My desire to save the world was also informed and supported by my beliefs about 'Oneness Philosophy.' Many people who connect to the sense of oneness feel driven to save the world because they can see and feel that the world's suffering is their suffering. They also totally understand that the world's enlightenment is their enlightenment – that unless everyone raises their consciousness, none of us do. That last part is, of course, true. However, if we aren't looking after ourselves in the process of bringing love to the world, if we are not happy and joyful in the process, well then we're not bringing anything of worth to life.

Social evolution works best when it flows from love, not when we are pushing from despair. If we are taking on the world's problems and fighting against what is, this is spiritual activism and it is simply another form of violence. Another way of bringing NO to a world that would be much better served with a YES. This is discussed in more detail in the FreeMind Purpose Section (see page 214), but for now it's worth noting that our spiritual practices need to be balanced or they can take us off-center even further.

* **Unbalanced Pillar 1** Peace practices can lead to spiritual bypass.
* **Unbalanced Pillar 2** Power practices can lead to spiritual materialism.

* **Unbalanced Pillar 3** Purpose practices can lead to spiritual activism.

When I stopped my private practice I lost a significant part of what kept me balanced. I didn't realize at the time how much my work with clients kept me deeply connected to a source of balanced peace, power, and purpose. Every time I hypnotized a client, I too was connecting and refreshing my faith and harmony. Without that, I was slowly adrift without even realizing. So, I was inspired and driven by the FreeMind Principles but no longer connecting directly with the FreeMind Experience. Had I stayed connected, my faith would have been real and living. Instead it became theoretical and brittle. I became overly rigid and controlling of others and myself. My brow was furrowed and I was doing 'important' things.' I was SERIOUSLY trying to DO good.

It is no surprise that nothing was working. It was like trying to pull molasses uphill. Had I paid attention, I could have brought myself back into balance before things got worse. Unfortunately, I was so determined to succeed in exactly the way I had planned it (*ahem*), I didn't even realize how lost I was. I had lost my faith totally. I wasn't free and relaxed. I was gripping life far too tightly and everything was going wrong. In Chinese mythology, when things are out of balance, a dragon comes down to Earth and burns everything to the ground. Then the dragon's brother the phoenix, with its healing tears rises from the ashes.

MEETING MY DRAGON

'Let go of my hand,' he screamed, 'if you don't fucking let go, I will definitely kill you!' He loomed over me further, pressing his face into mine, threatening me with every aspect of his being. I could feel his wrist muscles flex as the grip of his hand tightened on the knife that he had against my throat. He screamed again at an incredible volume, 'LET FUCKING GO!' His breath and spit was all over my face. He really meant it. 'This is it,' I thought. 'This is how it ends. Foolish experimental therapist killed by his own client.'

I had been so sure of the FreeMind system, but now I was questioning everything. I felt my precious belief in my work ebb away further. His eyes were dead. Did I really think I could reach him? Was I so sure of this route to happiness? Was I certain it could apply to everyone? Every part of him exuded rage, death, and destruction. Even now, his breathing through his nose was wildly violent. He tilted his head even more threateningly and screamed in my face, 'GET YOUR FUCKING HANDS OFF OR I WILL FUCKING STAB YOU RIGHT HERE AND NOW!' He proceeded to make this point at the highest volume possible. I didn't let go. I couldn't let go. It seemed like the worst idea in the world.

He then bellowed the ultimate question at me. The words rang out and as I heard them I knew in that moment the universe was communicating to me. What a messenger! I don't think the universe could have come up with a more compelling mode of communication. He screamed into the core of my terror: 'YOU EITHER HAVE FAITH OR YOU DON'T. LET … FUCKING … GO …'

This was not about him anymore. I knew it. I had done

this to myself. The universe had run out of patience. I had no choice. This was about me, my life, and where I'd found myself. I had fallen so far from grace by trying to 'make things happen,' and now here was the universe holding a knife to my throat, compelling me to remember that I had to let go. The knife against my throat became a metaphor for me and I knew what I had to do. I had to let go of his wrist. Not in the faith that I wouldn't die – far worse than that. I knew I had to let go to the ultimate degree. I had to let go completely and accept that maybe it was time for me to die. I slowly, and with primal terror, released my fingers one by one and let him further press the knife into my neck.

This client was caught in a bipolar crisis where on the one hand he loved life and was inspired to engage with the world and be his very best (the manic up). On another level, he couldn't come to terms with all of the suffering in the world and ultimately that he and all his loved ones were, one day, going to die (the depressive crash). He couldn't bear it and he desperately wanted to not love life. He wanted to discount it and dismiss it. He was desperately trying to connect to the salvation of the cynical mind. He wanted the relief of the uncaring heart, laughing without a care in the suffering world, but he simply couldn't get to that sorry shore. He couldn't make that empty cynicism stick, so he did his best to amplify his darkness, to deepen his loathing. He didn't want to stop at the island of the broken-hearted, disconnected, and uncaring skeptic. No, he wanted to journey to the capital metropolis of NO. He wanted to tear it all down. He wanted to stop briefly at the pit of nihilism and dive down into the freedom of being a total psychopath.

I was totally captivated by the idea that I could save this client. I thought I was there to save him. As it turns out, he was there to save me. He didn't stab me but he did knock me out and stamp on me. What I felt was a feeling akin to being beaten round the head by a large cymbal. With the first blow, the whole side of my head seemed to explode in sound and agony. It felt as though I'd been hit and flattened by something moving at the speed of a train at full pelt. I lost consciousness immediately only to be brought round by him stamping on my head. Both blows became one, so it felt as though the one strike had me instantaneously on the floor. It was like being hit by something moving at the speed of light.

This was my dragon of chaos burning everything to the ground, so that harmony could reemerge. I knew instantly the lessons in the middle of that experience. The denial of my own needs and boundaries (spiritual bypass), the idea that there was a problem to be fixed (spiritual materialism), and the feeling that it was my responsibility to save the world (spiritual activism) became totally clear to me. I was totally out of balance and all of that was represented in my willingness to continue to work with this client who had threatened me before. I put myself in danger, to save him because I should and I was the only one who could. What a story that was!

This incident forced me to explore deeply the degree to which I would subjugate my needs for another. The blows to my head had been powerful enough to fill my inner eye with blood and nearly detach my retina. There was a moment when the doctors thought I might lose my eye. Fortunately my retina was fine but my nervous system was absolutely shot. I was totally frazzled. I couldn't handle any stress at all.

This is where the phoenix of my understanding truly rose from the ashes. Until that point, I had no idea just how many of my boundaries were unprotected – suddenly they all came into sharp relief. I simply couldn't do anything that I didn't want to do. Anything uncomfortable became unbearable. Suddenly I was no longer willing to do a whole range of things that I had previously agreed to. The injury meant that I finally started protecting my boundaries and being honest with myself about who I was and what I wanted. In practical terms, this was the return of my love for myself. I was so busy loving everyone else that I had totally forgotten myself in the process. They say, 'Charity begins at home.' I now understand what that means.

I had to rebuild my life. Everything had become unbalanced and the blow to the head had woken me up. Bit by bit, I redrew my boundaries, and I dropped the idea that the world needed saving. I stopped pushing to make businesses better places to work. I stopped working with clients who were seriously troubled, unable to pay, or dangerous. I allowed myself to start getting paid for my work again. I stepped away from relationships that didn't nurture me, and worked on making my life beautiful again. I no longer validated myself by the 'good' works that I had been doing. Instead I focused on feeling good, having fun, and living in happy and healthy ways.

This whole process was an incredible blessing because when I lost everything and nothing was working, I discovered that I had a conditional relationship with myself. I realized that previously I loved myself because I was good, effective, successful, popular, and so on. When I lost everything I didn't like myself. Rebuilding my life and my faith was first about being able to love myself deeply without any of that stuff. I had to develop a truly 'unconditional' love for myself.

As soon as I did these things, everything started falling into place again. Life started flowing again. This is what brought Pillar 3 of the FreeMind Experience into full clarity. Previously my 'purpose' had all been about charitable contribution and selfless service to others. I thought my purpose or social responsibility was to make the world a better place by doing good deeds. Now, I realized that our only responsibility, and the best way to contribute to the world, is much more about simply being our authentic selves and being truly happy.

In all your practices it is essential that you love yourself first.

It is essential that you remember this *before* you start to use the FreeMind Practices. If you want to make the world a better place, make YOUR world a better place. Enrich your life, bring joy to your heart, and light up your life. Then you are fulfilling your destiny. That is your only responsibility. That is your purpose. On hearing that, you might worry that you could then become an awfully selfish person. As far as I can tell, when we love ourselves first properly, we become much more lovely to be around and everything falls into place. A 'free mind' is a full heart and a full heart leads all things to love, freedom, and happiness.

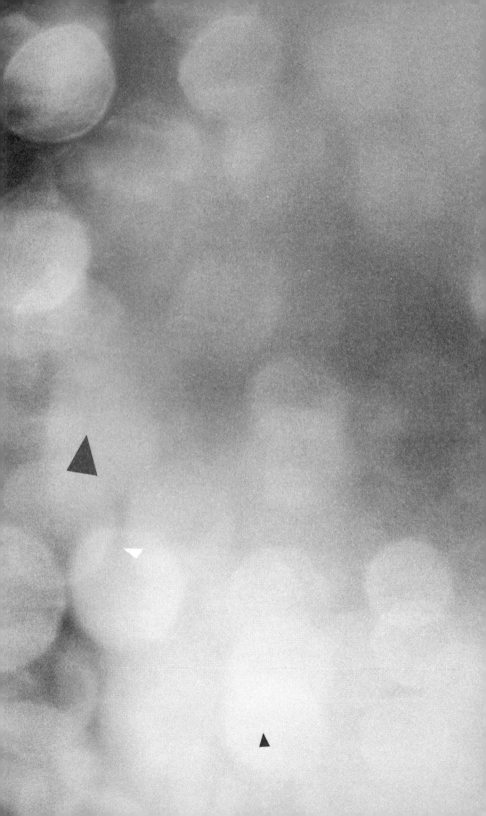

PART 2

THE FREEMIND PRINCIPLES AND PRACTICES

'Experience is not what happens to a man, it is what you do with what happens that counts.'

Aldous Huxley

Introducing the Three Pillars

Part II looks at each of the FreeMind Pillars in much greater detail. I have called them 'pillars' because it is upon these foundations that all lasting happiness and success are built. It is much harder to enjoy life when we are not deeply connected to our peace, power, and purpose. In each pillar, there are specific principles that I will explore in theory and then demonstrate how they can be applied. Throughout, you'll find examples from my own experiences and some interesting case studies[4] and relevant experiments.

At the end of each pillar there are a number of FreeMind Practices that you can use to help you start enjoying more peace, power, and purpose in your life.

These tools will first enable you to find your own NO moments and then help you to dissolve them. Doing the exercises can really help you to connect very deeply to a sense of YES about everything that has ever happened to you. That is the first YES.

That then enables you to be fully accepting and loving of yourself as you are. It means you will be able to be fully present, meeting the moment complete in your own power.

That is the second YES.

When you can meet the moment in that way, it will open your heart to the whole of life. You will be able to love all things unconditionally. That is the third YES.

The FreeMind Experience is the Triple YES to life. By the end of this process, you will be fully at PEACE, completely in your POWER, and therefore beautifully fulfilling your PURPOSE.

FreeMind Peace: Deprogramming

FreeMind Peace is not about continuously walking around with a simpering smile on your face, enjoying endless happiness. It is not unending joy. You will still get angry, depressed, frustrated, jealous, and insecure. All of these emotions will move through us at times. Peace comes from developing your emotional fitness. Physical fitness is measured by the speed with which your heart rate returns to its resting rate once it has been pumping at full pelt. Emotional fitness is the speed with which you return to peace and love once you have been upset, scared, and angry. How quickly can you bring yourself back from an adrenalin-fueled, fight-and-flight response? That is the question.

Fortunately, just like physical fitness, emotional fitness can be developed with exercise and practice. The practices, described at the end of this chapter (see page 115), are designed to start this healing process and can transform your relationship with life, no matter what difficulties or problems have been thrown at you.

DEPROGRAMMING AND EMOTIONAL INTELLIGENCE

Our capacity to return to peace rapidly after getting upset is hugely dependent on the degree to which we have cleared out all of our old upsets and resentments. As a result of a history of NO moments, most of us have large stores of negative emotions, resistances, and frustrations. As I described earlier (see Chapter 3, page 31), most of us are intrinsically in opposition to ourselves and the natural process of life and death.

All of these negative emotions and limiting ideas hold us back and massively skew our perception of the world. This often results in living in impoverished and unfulfilling ways, where we needlessly struggle and suffer. Before we can go on to experience more freedom and happiness in our lives, we must first systematically go through a process of deprogramming any thoughts, feelings, beliefs, and identities that are blocking our ability to be happy. This is all about bringing peace to our inner world. The driving force in FreeMind Peace is Emotional Intelligence.

With Emotional Intelligence it is clear that deprogramming and coming back to peace isn't about condemning any part of you or pushing aspects of yourself away. This, in fact, is more about bringing love and compassion to every part of you and your life. It is about letting your defense mechanisms know that you are finally ready to know the truth. It is about:

* Thinking every thought that was once too difficult to think.
* Feeling the feelings that were once too difficult to feel.

* Saying the things that were once too difficult to say.

This process isn't about making you feel bad about yourself but rather reassuring all those frozen parts of yourself that you are safe now. Using the FreeMind Peace Practices (see page 115), you can work through your uppermost layers of NO, and this will help you to:

* Directly secure, support, and see your whole self with love (re-parenting, see also Chapter 3, page 31).
* Bring yourself back into alignment with the vibration of YES.

When this work is successful, we typically begin to feel gratitude for everything that has ever happened to us. This is no longer about acceptance and forgiveness. It goes way beyond that. We begin to see that everything that has ever happened to us is an essential part of who we are. We begin to see how we are a part of everything in the world, and that everything in the world is part of us. We are intrinsically part of the flow of life. We have trust or what some people may refer to as faith. We are peaceful and fear no longer has the same hold on us. By some descriptions this is all about approaching life from a more enlightened perspective.

In Buddhism, one description of enlightenment translates as extirpation of fear. Extirpation is extinguishing a flame by removing the fuel or substance on which it burns. So, instead of blowing out a candle, the oxygen in a room would be sucked out. Without any external or internal force, the flame simply fades and disappears. Extirpation of fear and resistance comes from the gentle dissolving of the NO state.

UNFINISHED BUSINESS: HOW NO STATES INVITE TROUBLE ON PURPOSE

NO states tend to attract situations or people to us that match the feelings that we are holding on to. This, I believe, is a psychological explanation behind the concept of *karma*. There is no separate and vengeful or punishing and rewarding divinity. There is simply this beautiful and perfect field of balance: Imbalance always seeks resolution. The field (us) wants to be free of any sense of holding or resistance. When we experience something that we consider to be 'bad' or 'unpleasant' or 'not wanted' many of us resist the experience. We may tense up, switch channels, drink another beer, ignore the feelings, or indulge in any number of other ways of saying 'NO' to the experience.

In bigger moments of disappointment, pain, or trauma, these emotions are sometimes totally pushed out of our conscious awareness. This is due to our inbuilt understanding that it is necessary to shelve some of our more crippling concerns in order that we can get on with life. This coping mechanism starts in childhood, when our unconscious knows that thinking our parents or caregivers can't actually meet our needs is threatening and toxic.

Andy White describes this in his wonderful book *Going Mad to Stay Sane*. He explains, and I have experienced this in my private practice many times, that we would rather think less of ourselves than think less of our caregivers. This is not out of some sense of love or duty. It is simply that at a younger age, feeling this way is the lesser of two evils. Yes, thinking 'I am bad' or 'I am inadequate' is very destructive to our ability to succeed in life, love, friendship, and business, and so on, but all that comes later. When you are seven, thinking your parents are not safe is far too terrifying, so it is better to blame yourself for their failings.

As humans we are born with an innate desire for closeness with our parents. It is part of our survival mechanism programming, and runs so deeply within us that the skin-to-skin contact between a parent and a premature baby can greatly improve their chances of survival. As we develop, if we are lucky, we receive plenty of affection from our parents in the form of verbal and physical love. As children, we ache for these basic validations and know that something is 'wrong' if they are missing. We also know intuitively that brutality, abuse, or neglect are also things that don't feel 'right.'

However, the idea that our main caregivers are not 'safe' or, worse, are 'bad' is an incredibly toxic can of worms that most of us would rather not open. In fact, we will do pretty much anything to avoid thinking those thoughts. This is not about some sense of loyalty; it is simply about survival. Young children don't usually suffer with nervous breakdowns, not because they are not at risk or in danger from careless or abusive parents, but because they delude themselves. Having unsafe parents is a truly terrifying thought that could lead to a complete meltdown, so we have to make sense of what is going on, while also hanging on to some belief that our parents are safe.

In psychology this is called 'idealization.' We believe, no matter what, that they are OK. That makes us feel better, which is good, but how we do that can cause serious trouble for us later on in life. Unpicking this idealization is key to Pillar 1 of FreeMind. Without resolving this, nothing else works. Now, obviously these challenges are much more pronounced in people with really difficult histories but in my experience this stuff is operational in everyone to some degree. Even the simplest of interactions with a momentarily distracted parent can lead a child to believe that there is something wrong with them.

PAIN IS ALWAYS AN AS YET UNHEARD MESSAGE OF FREEDOM

Quite often, we deal with these scary feelings by ignoring them. Of course, this doesn't resolve the feelings; it simply stores them deep within our unconscious. Fortunately, although it may not always feel that way at the time, all those shelved feelings act like a magnet, attracting similar people and situations toward us. These people or situations trigger our discomfort, which makes us aware of the pain that we are holding on to from our past. In my work with clients, I find that everything that frustrates or upsets them about their 'present' holds up a mirror to a time in their past when they had experienced the same feelings but hadn't fully dealt with them. What an opportunity!

So, if all anguish, upset, anxiety, jealousy, hatred, disgust, and so on are signs that we need more freedom and love, then by actually allowing yourself to feel these emotions, you can release all the tension and negativity – which you may have been storing away for years. Unfortunately, most people don't make a practice of feeling these emotions and bringing them to light.

....

THE POWER OF REGRESSION

One of the reasons I became interested in hypnotherapy was because a hypnotherapy recording had a very powerful effect on me when I was younger. Despite being very skeptical at the time, I think I was expecting to experience some kind of zombie state where I would have no memory of anything that happened, but no such magic occurred. After a few minutes, I did feel relaxed but certainly not hypnotized according to my (wholly inaccurate) expectations. Anyway, I went along with the hypnotherapist's suggestions and visualized a big movie screen. While I couldn't picture this clearly, I got a sense of what was supposed to be happening.

Next, he asked me to think of a time when I could have used more support. I couldn't help rolling my eyes and thinking, 'What nonsense,' but sure enough a memory did pop up in my mind. But this memory was nothing. It was a tiny detail, I was seven or something and it was no major trauma. It was a memory of a time when I didn't feel heard, and I felt misunderstood by my parents. I remembered it well and I was just being a needy little kid; I was being daft, it was nothing. I would have much preferred to have some dramatic meaty mayhem to work on. But no, I thought of some minor childish whine.

The hypnotherapist invited me to step into the memory and despite all pronounced internal resistance something absolutely stupefying happened. I imagined stepping into that memory and in the midst of all my doubts, judgments, and criticisms, a tear rolled out of my right eye and I was shellshocked into silence. It felt as though my heart had quietly gasped and I'd stopped breathing. All my cynicism disappeared and I immediately felt into what I was feeling. To my surprise I discovered that everything I had just said about that memory, was everything I said to myself at the time. I wasn't being a stupid little kid. What had happened was really significant. I wasn't heard, my needs weren't met and it was the first moment that I realized that my parents weren't actually getting it right with me.

That moment revealed some wider concerns I had about my feelings about my parents. Back then it was a really scary moment because my fears about my parents were too toxic for me to dwell on, so I immediately denied them. I told myself I was just being a stupid kid, I was being pathetic, they were right to ignore me, and I shouldn't have mentioned anything. A distant part of me closed down in some small way to myself that day; a part of me became less willing to speak up about my needs; a tiny part of me lost some faith that the world and my place in it was OK.

....

So many of our big upsets come from the toddler or child inside us who is still just moments away from falling to the floor and having a four-limb-flailing tantrum. Such things are rarely that far away, if we scratch the surface. And let's be clear, I think I was hugely lucky with my childhood. I think on balance my parents did a good job. Most of the scarring and damage was done incidentally. I have helped many people overcome much bigger challenges created by parents who were directly destructive, neglectful, and abusive.

Connecting with your younger self and letting yourself feel everything that you once would have been too scared to feel is liberating. It is also the essence of Pillar 1. Finding all those moments of NO in your life and being honest with yourself, so you can feel the feeling and no longer tell yourself that you are stupid, less than, inadequate, unworthy, or deserving of being ignored or hurt.

When you are courageous enough to commune deeply with all of your past, it feels as though a massive burden has been lifted off you. You might feel more relaxed, whole, and adult. This is because, when we repress feelings, a part of us remains stuck at that age, frozen in time. When the repressed feelings are brought to light, you are able to give them the benefit of your adult perspective – they are able to age, grow up, and be integrated back into your adult life. We are also able to recognize that sometimes our interpretation of a parent's behaviors was inaccurate. What we may have seen as a lack of love because they were too busy to play with us, may actually have been them doing their very best to work hard to keep a roof over our heads and pay the bills. With an adult perspective we are able to see love working in many more ways.

LIBERATION FROM LIMITATION: YES!

The most amazing thing about the human spirit is resilience. We are all ultimately able to decide what our life means, to decide what our past means, to choose the reaction that we want to define us. To revisit all of our NOs and find what beauty and opportunity lies in all of them. To move through all the true layers of pain and anguish without defense, without feeling the need to change our past. To have the capacity to feel every last morsel of every last experience, not as some nightmare to be endured but as a pure rich source of the most divine opportunity to be free. The freshest, most enlivening, and exquisite sense of aliveness comes when we have the courage to face our truths without defense.

When we do this, we are liberated from limiting ideas, which pull us away from love and happiness. We dissolve all the fearful, closed, and cold feelings preventing us from being who we truly are. By accepting yourself, you say 'YES' to the experience. By this, I don't mean a begrudging acceptance, but a celebration of everything that has brought you to where you are today.

When you are 100 percent at peace with everything that has brought you here today – seemingly good and bad – then you can be at peace with yourself and be your best, most loving self.

This is true freedom. In this place, every limp becomes a new dance, every scar a new lesson, every loss a new compassion, every cruelty a new strength, and every challenge a new understanding. In this place, we are free. In this place we are connected to the creative power of the universe and then all we really feel is awe and gratitude. I know clients have truly healed when, if given the choice, they would choose to have their life exactly as it was. This is the ultimate healing – when you would choose to have the pain exactly as it was. When you can see an intrinsic and interdependent connection between your pain and your greatness, when you can see no delineation between what someone else might call good or bad, then you begin to understand that you are everything that you have ever experienced.

To want any part of our past to be different is to reject ourselves in the process, to reject life in the process, and imagine that somehow the world has made a mistake. It feeds the whole idea that something is wrong, that something is broken, that you *need* to be different or that the world *needs* to be different. There is no peace in this. There is only suffering and struggle. Whereas seeing all things as part of the beautiful, interconnected, and interdependent whole frees us to flow with life rather than against it. This is the Triple YES of absolute happiness.

LEARNING TO FLOW AND CO-CREATE WITH WHAT IS

Some people might argue that simply accepting the 'slings and arrows of outrageous fortune,' as Shakespeare so famously quipped, is impossible when, for example, watching a loved one suffer. However, if someone you care about deeply is struck down by some awful arrow then being free will also mean behaving in the best way possible at that moment.

This total acceptance of the 'All,' or Triple YES is not an empty, cold, and disassociated relationship to life – quite the opposite. When you are at peace with life as it is, you have the capacity to be truly there, to be fully present, to feel total love, adequacy, openness, confidence, integrity, and courage. You are therefore much more likely to flow with brilliant excellence and be the most supportive, innovative, and caring friend, lover, or parent. These are the qualities of an open heart — a free mind.

Railing against our bad luck or what life has thrown at us, we are lost in fear, contracted, suffering, resistant, tense, restricted, clumsy, inefficient, and blocked creatively. I know who I would rather have at my side in times of difficulty. Accepting 'what is' is not an empty passive process. We are the co-creator of 'what is' and flowing with that is empowering.

When we flow with a sense of YES to 'what is,' we respond in a fresh way to each moment and so deliver exactly what each situation requires of us. If we are not free in the moment, nothing flows, everything is a struggle, and we have to push to get out of our own way. With that said, it is possible that you feel pretty good about things. You may feel OK with life as it is. You may have accepted your parents, come to terms with your body, forgiven others, and so on — but you may still have a bunch of repressed memories of upset and anguish, outside your conscious awareness, which are still burning white-hot with searing NO energy. Bringing these past resistances to life will release their negative energy and transform them into learning and peace, and so help you toward feeling fully peaceful, present, and alive.

The most beautiful thing to discover is that our darkest fears and upsets are actually powerful insights and guidance that are waiting to be understood. In some cases, it is the most powerful aspects of our selves waiting to be integrated.

SELF-PROTECTION

Sue's father struggled with depression and wasn't a super-attentive or loving parent. As already discussed, the most popular defense is self-blame (that is, 'It's not them, it's me' – see pages 41–6). The second favorite, which Sue chose, is: 'This is not bad, it is NORMAL. That's just what adults or parents do.' Feeling unsafe with her father was unbearable for Sue as a young child, so she told herself, 'It's hard being a grown-up, it's normal to struggle,' and 'Mental illness is really complicated and very hard to overcome.' What's more, to protect herself from rejection and disappointment, she developed the belief, 'He would love me if he could but he can't.'

When I met Sue, as an adult in her early forties, she was crippled by overpowering anxiety, emotionally frozen, totally unable to complete work projects, felt trapped, conflicted, and was convinced that something was wrong with the way her brain worked. Doctors confirmed she was bipolar and she was told she would have to stay on medication for the rest of her life. She was really frustrated with herself and full of self-loathing.

Once, when she was in a deep hypnotic state, I invited her to realize that there was nothing wrong with her, that in fact her self loathing and fear were all part of a 'This is really normal and difficult to overcome' belief system, so that she could avoid being honest with herself about her true feelings about her father. At last the little girl in her was able to face the true weight of disappointment and frustration she felt about her father not being the warm, playful, positive, and loving presence that he should have been to her.

Breaking down into tears, she sobbed, broke open, and for once was able to hold herself with love and compassion. She was filled with an overwhelming sense of relief that she was not actually mentally ill, or 'broken in my head,' as she described it. Her head was working very well. Feeling the feelings and thinking the thoughts that she never allowed herself to do as a child, changed her whole sense of self and her perception of life. The 'cure' therefore was to let her inner mind know that she wanted to know everything – she wanted to feel everything. No stone left unturned.

....

In Sue's case, the FreeMind Peace Process (page 117) helped her to connect to how disappointed and angry she was with her father, and helped her get beyond all the excuses she'd made for him. Those excuses had become beliefs that locked her problems in place. We also had to get beyond her forgiveness of him, which she'd worked on feeling for him through meditation and her spirituality. As I mentioned earlier (see page 98), you can't fully forgive until you have been honest with yourself about the degree to which you are actually still upset. Otherwise it prevents the truth of the real emotions being felt and released. She had been using her peaceful spiritual practices to bypass the truly painful feelings. This was actually blocking her ability to be happy.

Once we feel the truth, we no longer need to defend against it by telling ourselves 'They [our parents or caregivers] had no choice' or 'It is really difficult and complicated.' Dropping the idea that it is complicated or normal, we can allow things to change very rapidly. This is freedom. Returning to balance and sweet alignment takes time. But most of our troubles are not due to our personality or our minds. Our difficulties come from our refusal to commune with our darkest and most challenging thoughts and feelings.

ANALYSIS AND THE DEPARTURE FROM YES!

Many people think analysis involves years of regular sessions of lying on a couch talking while the therapist solemnly nods at you. However, analysis is not some unfortunate but necessary part of the process. It is an access point to the richest gold. It is the listening to the frozen and broken parts of our selves. It is the reintegration of some of our most powerful, playful parts and gives us a chance to come fully into balance. Understanding where our behaviors come from is vital because it is in the understanding that we can see the pattern and so pinpoint where we departed from YES. We can see where we have departed from our truth, what we have covered up, where we have denied our needs, and fallen out with life and love.

Mapping our defenses, feeling into the consequences, and forgiving ourselves for our attempts to protect ourselves is the key. When we can see what we have been doing and why we have been doing it, the self-attack falls away. Sue's brain wasn't broken; it loved her, it loved her father; it wanted her to be happy — it wanted her still to be able to feel warmly toward him. This is not dysfunction. This is love in action. OK, the mechanism was out of date, and it meant that she was experiencing profound self-sabotage but it was still all coming from love.

Now, that is a realization worth getting excited about. That is the real deal, and when you get that understanding for yourself it underpins your understanding of everyone else who is struggling in the world too. You can see into the hearts of everyone else, and their darkness turns from what may once have looked like evil into fear. Their brokenness now appears as a beautiful opportunity for freedom. Other people's challenges turn up as simply a calling for more love. True understanding is not just cold, cerebral, and theoretical analysis. When we have journeyed into our darkness and found love and protection at the root of our most pronounced problems, we can't help but feel love and compassion for other people who are lost and struggling.

....

PHOBIA OF CHILDREN

The way the brain protects us from pain is endlessly fascinating. At times, it builds models of the world on assumptions, which can then go on to shape so many critical choices in our lives. Take, for example, 55-year-old Lily, who came to me for help because she had a phobia of children. As with most fears, they grow if we don't confront them. This is doubly true of phobias.

Lily went from not liking teenagers to being absolutely petrified of them. She was embarrassed by her phobia and, inevitably, it was extremely debilitating because she just couldn't avoid them. There are, of course, many therapeutic techniques to help people overcome fears very quickly; for example, a single 60-minute session of neuro-linguistic programming (NLP) or emotional freedom technique (EFT) is usually sufficient to help someone overcome their fears. I am trained in those techniques and often use them to help people dissolve conditioned fear responses, but only after spending some time looking at why people are feeling fear and resistance (the Why?). Fears and phobias, like everything else, don't turn up without a beautiful (perfect) reason.

Once in a hypnotherapeutic trance, Lily remembered a truly sad time in her life when she was little. Her father had left her mother to bring up Lily and her two siblings alone. Her mother struggled financially but was determined that her children didn't grow up feeling poor. She did everything that she could to provide for their needs, never once complaining that money was short. Her mother believed that her children knowing money was short would be damaging, so she worked every hour she could. At the time, the three children, and Lily particularly, had no idea how tough it had been on her mother. That is, until she reached 18 when her mother had a breakdown due to the stress of trying to keep them afloat. All the financial troubles came out, and she was horrified to discover how hard her mother's life had been.

Her mother had made so many sacrifices, and all Lily could think of was all the times she had hassled her for new shoes and fashionable clothes. Being 'unaware' of their situation and 'oblivious' to the strain she had put on her mother was, in her mind, devastatingly 'inconsiderate.' This lack of awareness broke Lily's heart. She was so earnestly disgusted by her behavior that she couldn't really face herself. All she could do to protect herself from the guilt was to blame it on her youth. So, instead of hating herself, she hated her youthful ignorance. So it is no surprise that, years later, this fear and hatred overran. Her phobia was a projection of her self-loathing onto children in general.

Lily's freedom came in the true forgiveness of herself and the pulling back of that projection, so that she could see children afresh. When I use the word 'perfect' to describe this wonderfully balanced world we live in, I don't mean that things are not brutally painful. What I want to draw attention to is the fact that our separation from truth always brings perfectly symmetrical problems to our door. The problems are real (and sometimes horrible) but they are still part of the perfectly balanced process.

....

Lily's story highlights the value of exploring the 'Why?' To have simply fixed her 'problem' with a rapid-change technique would have missed the point completely. Symptoms can be 'swished' (a popular NLP phobia technique) away but all too often the symptom 'message' seeks expression in other ways. This can lead to more pronounced anxiety and depression or can all too often turn up later on in life as a physical disease. True understanding is the key to healing.

COMPLAINING AND COMPENSATING

When we are limited and fearful, we are often at the mercy of a sort of internal 'personality general' that takes command by vacillating between complaining and compensating. We develop these skills in the following ways to make ourselves feel OK and in control but, despite being useful, they can cut us off from the very love and happiness we are seeking:

Complaints (our victimology) are our judgments of ourselves, other people, and the world in general. They prevent us from feeling pain but also stop us taking full responsibility for our life. When we let the pain go, we can learn valuable lessons and then move on all the richer for it. Therefore, repetitive complaining about the past can become a deep grumbling pit of negativity, which blocks out all the light from our life.

Compensations are our behaviors, and at times valuable skills, which we have developed to survive. Examples of these behaviors might include being highly skilled in a certain task or being very self-reliant, independent, or being a highly productive or creative individual. Of course, these skills have huge merits, but it might serve to notice if those default behavior settings are on automatic and are preventing us from responding to life in the best way possible. For example, if 'being independent' is an automatic response, then it may be very hard to really let love in. We may struggle with allowing ourselves to be looked after. We may push away certain people and keep ourselves isolated.

Complaining and compensating really get in the way of making the most of life because we behave in ways that are, fearful, judgmental, distant, competitive, cruel, incongruent or, at the very least, inauthentic. This makes living a happy life impossible. FreeMind Peace is all about deprogramming our negative feelings and the resultant limiting beliefs and behaviors. This is as much about cleaning up your outer world (how you behave with other people) as it is about cleaning up your inner world (how you feel).

Once we have dissolved our fears and resentments we find ourselves wanting to live with honesty and authenticity.

To do this properly we naturally want to engage in a series of courageous conversations in which we apologize for our inauthenticity and do what needs to be done to make amends. I call this cleaning up.

CLEANING UP AND DROPPING JUDGMENTS

The whole point of a 'clean-up' courageous conversation is to get your side of the street clean. If you are hoping to have a loving conversation that will make the 'other' person be different, then that's missing the point. When we truly understand why everything has happened, we are no longer just coming from a place of forgiveness and acceptance. When we truly get it, we are simply grateful.

This process can take some time and, until that time, your communications may simply come over as attacks. No parent or loved one can easily hear the 'truth,' if what you are really saying is, 'I wish you hadn't done this' or 'I wish you could be different with me now.' What this communicates is, 'You are wrong and I am broken because of what you did (or didn't) do.' In truth, the degree to which you are broken is nothing to do with what they did or didn't do. It is all to do with what you have *made* their treatment mean to you.

When we own the story and the beliefs that we made up about our past, the real problem becomes clear − it is our resentments and frustrations that are the problem. Our interpretation is where the breakdown is occurring. At that point, we realize that the other person − being exactly as they are − has afforded us an opportunity to have the life that we have. That life is obviously a divine opportunity to experience life in all sorts of powerful, beautiful, and meaningful ways. It doesn't always involve things being easy, but that isn't where our character gets its best development. When we truly 'get' the beauty of life we want to let go of the complaining and compensatory (victim) thinking we have woven around our identity.

The leading principle of Emotional Intelligence says our feelings are our responsibility. No one else can make us feel anything.

I have seen long-term disputes miraculously dissolved by one person changing their position. All relationships consist of two people dancing in a certain way. You can't change your dance without affecting the other person. It is impossible. At the same time, it is very common for the other person to accept the apology (and or owning of the inauthenticity) and then say something like, 'Finally, I am glad you see the errors of your way. You have been a real pain in the ass. I accept your apology gratefully.' This can be pretty tough if all along, underlying your apology, there is a parched and anguished sense of 'But what about your part?' To do this with total authenticity, it really can't be about making the other person different, or winning, or getting your point across. This is simply about you returning to love. This is about your own freedom.

HOW THINGS CAN CHANGE WORDLESSLY

Harvey came to see me because he was struggling with some challenging emotions around women. He had grown up with a domineering and bullying father. His mother had been loving but never really stood up to his father. Harvey was angry about this, and had developed a defensive belief about his mother. He unconsciously chose to believe that instead of her being a letdown, she was actually just 'stupid.' The belief helped but to make this defense less painful (because no one wants to believes their parents are 'stupid'), he then normalized that belief across all women and imagined (albeit unconsciously) that all women were 'stupid.'

This defense mechanism worked until he became an adult and began to find all women infuriating. He didn't trust them or feel safe with them, and deep down he didn't believe they could really be there for him. This resulted in a pattern in which he was drawn to unavailable women, and meant that he was incredibly dismissive and patronizing toward them.

When I was working with him, he found a critical memory of a time when his father aggressively shoved his face into his supper. It didn't hurt, but it was violent and humiliating. As he described the feeling of food being all over his face, emotion welled up in him. His mother wasn't stupid but she'd been too scared to stand up to his father, and so had let Harvey down. He connected with the feeling and then began to let it all out. He felt the wound of that disappointment and was able to reassure his younger self that he was now safe because he was no longer dependent on these people for anything. He sobbed and let it all out, and even though it was very emotional and painful, within it he found huge relief. Now, he was able to see how he had been wanting to believe that all women were stupid, instead of really feeling the degree to which he was upset because his mother had not been there for him. As that upset and resentment was released, his heart softened and all of the real love he felt for his mother moved into the space. He was much more relaxed and philosophical about it all.

Harvey looked calm and peaceful. He realized that he had been very angry with his mother. Despite feeling let down by her, he knew how and why that had happened, and now he just felt huge amounts of compassion and love for her. He really wanted to apologize to her and to work on improving that relationship. We agreed to work on that in the next session. Apologies and reconciliation conversations need to be managed very carefully, otherwise the other person can still come away feeling criticized and attacked.

Later that night, however, something amazing happened. Out of the blue, his mother called him up to say how sorry she was that she hadn't always been there for him when he was younger. She expressed grave regret for not having stuck up for him more. This was nothing short of a miracle for Harvey and he was very authentically able to take responsibility for (own) the anger and resentment that he had been holding on to for years, which had been limiting him and getting in the way of their friendship. When one person shifts, the other person can't stay in the old position.

....

CLEARING NEGATIVE EMOTIONS AND MAKING AMENDS

Many so-called black sheep of the family are actually the truth-bearers. They are the person holding all of the problems of the family. Everyone else is getting on with it, but one person just can't quite contain his or her dissatisfaction. They may be challenged in all their relationships, failing at work, trapped behind difficult emotional problems, suffering from debilitating physical ailments, possibly struggling with general rebelliousness, and possibly a number of problematic addictions.

On one level they are just dealing with the unresolved conflicts of the family. A beacon, if you like, of truth begging to be recognized. However, often these challenges and 'problems' are more of an unspoken criticism. It is as if someone chooses unconsciously to struggle so they are silently saying to the parents, 'Look what you did to me!' While it can be useful for a family to explore the feelings behind these resistances and rebellions, it is even more useful for the individual. As a result of this unresolved anger and upset many people sabotage their own success as an unconscious desire to protest. It causes those unresolved (black sheep) individuals so much unnecessary pain and suffering and it doesn't achieve anything.

> 'Anger is like drinking poison and expecting the other person to die.'
> Buddha

Clearing away all of the negative emotions and beliefs, dissolving the defense mechanisms, stepping beyond the personality-based coping strategies, and making amends by setting things straight is what FreeMind Peace is all about. This is the foundation of freedom. It is an ongoing process. At times some of those courageous conversations can be both the most challenging and the most beautiful experiences you will ever have. With every step closer that you take toward your transparent truth, the lighter and brighter you'll feel.

Sometimes it is important to make amends for some of the things that we did when we were out of integrity. This might involve confessing something to an old partner or apologizing for something you now regret. This can also be more practical. It could involve doing something for someone to make up for it. It could even be about paying for something to be repaired or changed. These acts are not done to assuage guilt, they are more about simply setting things straight. However, sometimes a big confession can be wholly unsettling and destabilizing for another person. Just because it might feel good for you doesn't mean you 'should' do it, so before you barge back into someone's life with a burning torch of truth, it's important to ask yourself the following three questions:

1. Is it necessary?
2. Is it helpful?
3. Is it kind?

Be responsible and careful with your acts of amendment. If you are not sure, seek the advice of friends or a mental health professional before you take action.

FREEMIND PEACE IS ABOUT FACING THE TRUTH

When we avoid our fears, we run the risk of living lives that are not the fullest expression of our greatest potential. Many people avoid their truth through continuous activity – such as overworking, being over-busy, keeping the TV on, always having something on the go, over-shopping, overeating, addictions, and various other ways – which prevent us from acknowledging the truth about how we feel about ourselves and our lives.

For example, I know many people who are dangerously addicted to powerful drugs, which they use to prevent them from realizing their true discomfort. They take uppers and downers every day just to manage life. They come in from work frazzled, stressed, upset, unhappy, and uncomfortable. If they spent time with those feelings they would probably be motivated to make a change in their life, but instead they take downers to 'take the edge off,' and then need large amounts of stimulants (uppers) to wake up their system the next day.

Alcohol and coffee are not really thought of as downers and uppers, and so go unnoticed as the drugs that they are. The playwright George Bernard Shaw said, 'Alcohol is the anesthetic required to handle the operation of life.' I think it's safe to say that alcohol is the anesthetic required to remain unaware that you may actually like to change your life.

To be clear, there are lots of people who have great lives, are very happy, and who also thoroughly enjoy drinking alcohol and/or coffee. That is, of course, fine. The point I am making is that there are lots of people who are unhappy, who use alcohol or other stimulants, food, TV, keeping busy, not stopping, not feeling, to hide from feelings that it might serve them to pay attention to. The problem is we cannot escape our miseries and nor should we want to. Our difficult emotions, if listened to, are the signposts back to our happiness.

Don't make your discomfort more bearable. Listen to it, amplify it, get in there, and listen to what your heart is saying.

Your heart may well be begging you to allow yourself to live a completely different life. If that is the case, every part of you will be so much happier once you've done that. And, in the long term, so will everyone else you are connected to. The transitions to truth can be incredibly painful and challenging but living a half-life is never any good for anyone.

LIVING IN A WORLD THAT FACES THE TRUTH

People run into real trouble when they deny their emotional difficulties and push away the darkest aspects of themselves. Our darkness festers and brews, and seeks resolution in all sorts of limiting and destructive ways. The only solution for those difficult parts of our selves is for them to be communicated with. The darkness needs to be brought to light and understood. Then it can be negotiated with and invited into new, more productive, and harmonious ways of being. Metaphorically, this is the same as when we lock away our problem people in prison.

Locking away our 'problems' isn't the answer for rehabilitation and locking away our negative emotions isn't the answer for our own emotional wellbeing. Nor is medicating them. That is just another kind of prison for our emotions. We don't need more pills and more walls. We need more understanding and integration. When we reintegrate an aspect of ourselves that has previously been repressed, we discover that these parts of ourselves actually have some incredibly valuable gifts and skills.

When you can truly meet, understand, and love every part of yourself, you drop the need for control. You can let go of the idea that you are not enough. You can begin to trust in a very deep way that you are the perfect person, with the perfect skills, turning up at the perfect time to do the perfect thing. No force, no pressure, no stress, and no doubt. This is FreeMind Peace and it is one of the core pillars upon which all happiness is built.

FreeMind Peace Practices

What follows are a number of exercises and practices that you can start to experiment with, to help you bring more peace into your life. These practices are designed to help you to become more loving of yourself and others. They will help you meet your present moment with more composure and openness. You may find that things won't bother you in quite the same way and you'll become less concerned about what other people think about you. FreeMind Peace is all about developing a deep appreciation for life and the capacity we all have in every moment to remember what a blessing it is to be alive.

Some of the exercises are practical things that you can do in your outer world; others are more about making changes in your inner world.

At the end of this section there is also a list of recommended resources that can support you in becoming more peaceful (see page 133).

....

USING THE FREEMIND PRACTICES

When using the inner FreeMind Practices, it is important that you make yourself comfortable before you start – for example, ensure that you won't be disturbed, and allow plenty of time to do the process completely. When doing these exercises it is normal for your mind to wander and it is fine for you to move around to keep yourself comfortable. If possible:

* Do the exercises with your eyes comfortably closed.
* Allow yourself to become very still (your ability to do that will improve over time).
* Just take note of what you notice. You may find that some parts of the exercise are easier than others, but these are not things that you can get wrong.
* Don't get frustrated with yourself or think that these experiences have to be anything in particular.
* Keep an open mind. It is normal to have doubts.
* Give each exercise at least two good attempts. You may also notice that, at times, certain exercises won't work at all for you. In this case, try a different exercise or repeat it at a later time and you may respond differently.

As you allow yourself to go on these inner FreeMind journeys more and more, you may notice strange sensations, such as heaviness or lightness, in your body. You may even feel as if you are going numb. These are all perfectly normal reactions. You can stop whenever you want and your body will rapidly return to its usual sensations.

Wherever possible, become curious about the physical effects of the exercises. They are usually very positive signs that you have become deeply relaxed, which has been proven to be very good for both mind and body.

Some of the practices may take some getting used to but feel free to make them work for you. Be patient, generous, and collaborative. Don't hope they will 'do' something to you. Work with them to help them help you.

....

FREEMIND PEACE PRACTICE 1

THE PEACE PROCESS

This process is one of the main practices for bringing more peace to your life, and has the potential to create more change than any other technique I have ever come across. This is the ultimate tool for going from NO to YES. Whenever you are feeling challenging emotions (NO) about your present, it is always a deeper calling to do more healing on your past (NOs). You can focus on a present-day upset and use it to explore your consciousness for old resistance. No doubt you will then find similar feelings from your past that you may have shelved (repressed) in your system because you were unable to deal with them at the time.

For example, you may feel angry with your boss or partner, and this might be a sign that there are deeper wounds triggering your emotional reaction. Taking the time to feel the feelings and track down the sources of any unfinished emotional business is a vital part of living a healthy, happy, and harmonious life. Discovering the source of your emotions may be difficult, but it is also a beautiful opportunity to bring peace into what was previously painful. Once you have learned to do this process, it is very easy to do it by yourself, but in the beginning you might want to ask a trusted friend to help talk you through it. You can also download a fully guided version of this process from www.freemindproject. org (see also FreeMind Resources, page 253).

1. If you're feeling upset or emotional, find a place where you can lie down, and won't be disturbed.

2. Become aware of your breathing and notice where your body is tense. Taking each area of tension in turn, focus on breathing into and relaxing that part of your body. Do whatever you can to be as still as possible while slowing down your breathing. To do this, consciously choose to breathe out for longer than you do usually. Pause before breathing in and then breathe in deeply and slowly. Try and savor each breath, making it last as long as possible. Don't worry if you find this difficult, it is not vital to feel totally relaxed. You might want to use some music to help you relax (see page 133).

3. Tell yourself that you are ready to feel and understand. You don't want to avoid any feelings. This is really about opening up to yourself. Like a parent (peacefully, lovingly, and without any fear at all) saying to a child that has just had a nightmare, 'Tell me all about it, darling.' This is about re-parenting yourself. Being able to meet old feelings that were once too difficult to feel. By showing yourself willing, you are reassuring those frightened younger parts of yourself that everything is OK now.

4. Start to sense where the emotion is coming from in your body and allow yourself to focus on feeling it. For example, do your stomach or shoulder muscles feel

tense? Are your hands clenched? Does your head feel tight or your throat dry? Just allow yourself to be upset or tense, and feel the emotion as fully as possible. Notice if a part of you wants to judge you or the feelings or the exercise. Do your best to welcome all of these feelings and judgments too.

5. Even though you may have a situation in your present-day life, which you feel is the source of this upset, let yourself know that you want to use this upset to find any other times in your past when you have felt a similar way. For example, you may be upset because a relationship has ended, you may be angry with your boss, or even stuck in traffic. Whatever is causing the upset is not important. You are going to use that upset to help you let go of old stuff that you are unnecessarily holding on to. Do this by simply concentrating on the feeling of the emotion in your body and then dropping the present-day story. Feel the emotion and stop focusing on the current situation. Notice and name the emotion you are feeling in your body. Is it fear, anger, guilt, a sense of loneliness, abandonment? Really feel into it and sense that you have felt this very same feeling before.

6. Feel the emotion as much as possible, making the feeling as big and welcome as possible. Let it expand in your awareness. Give it permission to be there. Do this by relaxing your body even more. When we feel these emotions it is common to tense up. That is your body's way of saying 'NO.' You are doing this exercise to let go of the fear and resistance – to bring it back to a YES. Do this by breathing into it, relaxing further, and being

willing to open up any old thoughts and feelings that may relate to it. Then tell yourself that you are going to count down from ten to one, and that when you do, your inner mind (or heart, unconscious, or soul) will help you remember, re-experience or re-feel any memories that are associated with this kind of feeling. This process lets your inner mind know that you are ready to become conscious of anything that may serve you to be aware of.

7. A part of you may feel very scared but this is completely normal. This fear is associated with your past response to the situation. Not the situation itself. Thoughts and feelings can be upsetting, but it is not feeling them that is the problem. It is all about having the courage to feel the feelings and think the thoughts that were once too scary to bring into your conscious. Pushing away your feelings only locks them in. Feeling them releases them, enabling us to come back into peace. This is you finally meeting your younger self. This is you loving yourself. This is you coming to terms with everything that has ever happened to you. This is you being like a loving parent to yourself. This is you coming back to peace.

8. Breathe deeply, feel the feelings and then start to count down from ten to one. At the count of one, just notice what you notice, give yourself space. Memories may come your way, difficult thoughts and challenging feelings may surface, but just stay with the process; keep breathing and do your best to be lovingly curious. Like listening to a child telling you about a bad dream. Most of the feelings will have been locked inside for a long time, preventing you from loving yourself and life. By feeling these feelings you are being there for yourself

in a way that means all sorts of beautiful changes can begin to occur naturally. Remember you are not feeling these emotions or thinking these thoughts to get rid of them. You are feeling them as an act of true expression. You are honoring them by allowing them to be present and fully felt.

9. Once you have explored and released feelings from one memory, you may want to spend some time imagining different versions of yourself at different ages (or specific memories you know were difficult) as you were growing up. If you do that, notice that there may be some feelings of rejection or blame between you and your younger self. This process is about bringing enough compassion and understanding to every part of yourself, so that peace and love can melt away the negative behavioral patterns in your life, allowing you to live and love your life to the full. It can sometimes take several sessions to form a deeply loving and positive relationship with your younger self. Take your time and work on that relationship as often as you can. Certainly don't feel bad or guilty about needing to work on that relationship. Just take it one day at a time.

10. To end this process, imagine bringing every part of you back into full integration. You might want to visualize cuddling the younger version of yourself. You might want to imagine that part becoming a ball of light that you can embrace and integrate into your chest/belly/ genitals/head. You might want to imagine that younger part of you is growing up inside you with all sorts of new resources and energy. When we cut off parts of ourselves we can also lose some of our natural gifts

like playfulness, spontaneity, and creativity. By giving space for all of us to be heard and felt, we can become more adult, more whole, and that can really bring us back to life with some wonderful skills. So for this part of the process, it can be lovely to listen to beautiful music that you love. Imagining that is the sound of you loving yourself and you connecting to your peaceful, loving potential more than ever before. Our biggest challenges are the source of our greatest powers. As you listen to this music, think about how some of the hardest experiences in your life have actually furnished you with some amazing gifts like compassion, understanding, and empathy.

11. When your healing is complete you will feel grateful for everything that has ever happened to you. Even the darkest of times will be seen as a vital part of what enables you to be your fully amazing self today. So, as a final part of this process, relax your body further, bring your attention to your physical body. Start with your toes and consciously move all the way up your body, finally bringing your attention to the front of your head. Take a moment to think about the gifts that you have received and the characteristics that you have developed along the journey of your unique life. The FreeMind perspective sees everything as interconnected and interdependent. Our greatest challenges are the source of our greatest gifts. Spend some time feeling into these connections and then do your very best to let everything be as it is. Be (or move toward being) sincerely grateful for everything. Essentially give your past your blessing. This is the best way to end this process and it is also the best

way to bring enormous amounts of love and peace to
your life.

This process can be very emotional and it is good to let everything move through you as much as possible. Just let it all
out. With that said, this process doesn't need to be loud and
dramatic. Very often tears will simply gently stream down
your face. At other times you will try and track your feelings
but nothing will come up, and the whole experience can
feel disconnected and contrived. Be gentle with yourself no
matter what happens, and let go of needing the experience
to look or feel in any specific way. It is worth persevering.
It can be also useful to record your experiences in a journal
afterward. Once the process is over, even though it is positive
and healing, you may still feel tired, drained, and quite raw.
You may be more likely to be more emotional for a while
afterward. Once this passes you will most likely feel really
grounded, alive, and much more whole.

FREEMIND PEACE PRACTICE 2

LIFE STORY: BRINGING LOVE TO LIFE

As you start to understand the interconnected nature of
everything, you'll find that you can't be grateful for one
thing in your life without being grateful for everything
else too. You can't resist parts of your past without resisting
part of who you are. By developing the practice of feeling
gratitude for everything, you can begin to feel complete love
and gratitude for who you are in the moment.

1. Start by making a list of everything that you are grateful for. If you find it difficult to think of anything, then start with the basics: The air you breathe, the warmth of the sun, your health, a happy memory, your favorite piece of music, and so on. If you think about it, you can be grateful for all sorts of things that most people simply take for granted. Ensure there are at least 25 things or people on your list – if you can get to a 100, that's fantastic.

2. Next, list everything in your life that has been challenging, difficult, and painful. Include anything that you might remember as being a 'bad experience' or trauma. Your NO list.

3. Pick one of those experiences and spend some time thinking about how that experience has (or could have) shaped you, and look for the (possible) positive characteristics, beliefs, and behaviors that have (or could have) come from it. Do this, in turn, with each of the experiences on your NO list. If you find one, or more, of them is too challenging then put it aside and, when you're ready, use FreeMind Peace Practice 1 (see page 117) to help you re-experience it.

4. Now, for each NO experience, write a description of how it could have actually been a valuable experience or a blessing in disguise. How has each one of those experiences shaped your life, or how could they help you live a more beautiful life?

5. When you have found a positive perspective or meaning within each one, take some time to feel gratitude for that experience. Do your best to become grateful for everything that has ever happened to you and, when

you're ready and it has been transformed, add that YES moment to your gratitude list.

FREEMIND PEACE PRACTICE 3

CLEANING UP

Using the first two Peace Practices above you get learning and insight, which can help you bring your life back into balance. You then really start to see those challenging times as an intrinsic part of what makes life good. When we see that fully, we can then see that all of our resistances and judgments have led to us withholding love and peace from ourselves and indeed everyone else too. To further put an end to these painful and unnecessary dynamics, you may feel driven to 'clean up' your life. To have some courageous conversations and make amends. This is really about bringing love back to life and it is a vital part of the FreeMind Peace.

To get beyond the complaining and compensating (victim) state discussed earlier in the chapter (see page 104), it can be a useful starting point to write a letter to anyone that you used to blame. More often than not, this will be directed to a parent or a primary caregiver. Of course, the letter doesn't need to be sent, because it is more about going through the process of diligently dissolving the idea that it is the other person's fault.

The clean-up letter isn't about attacking the other person. It is an unequivocal apology for any negative emotions that you have been holding on to, which may have been getting in the way of the relationship working. This is essentially about owning up to the inauthenticity of your feelings.

Apologizing for how you have been negatively affecting the relationship. This isn't about you talking about your 'part' so they apologize for their 'part.' This is nothing to do with them. When you can truly see that it is our fear that has been the problem, it is common to experience much more love and understanding for that person. Your whole energy can change and you may be drawn to send the letter or, more commonly, to have a truly authentic conversation with the person. This exercise prepares you for that conversation.

1. Enlist the help of a trusted (ideally wise) friend or therapy practitioner, and explain to them the purpose of cleaning up and letter writing. Discuss it, so that you are both totally clear that the process is not about attacking or judging other people. This is simply about you owning your own inauthenticity, your own withholding, and it is also (more often than not, but not necessarily) a statement of intent that you would like to be more open, loving, and connected to the person concerned.

2. Draft your apology letter and then ask your friend/ professional to read it, and look for any overt and covert words or phrases that directly, or indirectly, attack the person in question.

3. Repeat this process, until your letter is simply an authentic apology without any malice, anger, judgment, or resentment. Ensure there is no part of the communication that is suggesting or inviting the other person to be different or to do anything differently.

4. Once you and your friend/professional agree that the letter serves its intended purpose, you don't have to send the letter but you will have done the necessary

preparation to have a conversation with that other person if you choose. Some people like to begin that conversation by either reading the letter or simply apologizing from their heart. Remember that this exercise is not about getting them to change or even hoping that anything will change. This is simply about you bringing more love to that relationship. This is about you loving them exactly the way they are.

Real freedom doesn't come from us loving people because of who THEY *are. In our most free place, we love people because of who* WE *are.*

FREEMIND PEACE PRACTICE 4

A SIMPLER MESSAGE OF LOVE

Sometimes we don't want or need to go and clean up anything (see FreeMind Peace Practice 2, page 123). Sometimes we feel so much gratitude and love that we simply want to express it. No matter how difficult some of the people in our life may be (or have been in the past), it can be such a beautiful thing to simply send them some love. When we see things clearly, it is easy to see that all our (and their) negative behaviors come from fear. Fear doesn't deserve further attack. Only love dissolves fear and it can be such a beautiful thing to reach out to people with love; to drop our judgments and withholding, and simply express absolute love for them. Yes, birthdays and other special holidays are a good time to cherish our loved ones but there are plenty of other things that you could do today. Here are a few ideas to get you started:

* Send a loving text to an old friend right now.
* Go online and find the perfect gift for someone you care about or appreciate, or maybe surprise that person with a gift that is totally out of the blue.
* Send a love letter to a friend or a note of appreciation to a parent.
* Pop a delicious treat in a colleague's, your child's, or your friend's bag so they discover a lovely surprise later in their day.
* Slip a love letter into your partner's bag before they go on a trip.
* Take time to give someone special in your life a long loving hug.
* Transmit your love to everyone you meet by smiling and giving them your time, whether it's an elderly person on the bus, your colleagues, or your children.
* Surprise someone by doing something lovely for them. Repair or replace something, wash their car overnight, or help them with a project.
* Babysit for a parent so they can have a night off.
* Help a neighbor.
* Read to, or spend time listening to, an elderly person.
* Give blood.
* Volunteer at a shelter.
* Take a loved one on a magical day full of adventure. This doesn't have to be a grand and expensive gesture.
* Give some money to a homeless person.

* Do any random act of kindness.
* Take yourself out on a date. You know what you like. Make a whole day of it and pack it with things you love.

Taking the time to get beyond our usual patterns and history of resistance and pain to lovingly reach out and connect can be wholly healing and nourishing. Stop reading this book and do something beautiful for someone you love right now. Send one text to someone you love. Maybe someone you haven't spoken to for over a year. Tell them how important they are to you.

FREEMIND PEACE PRACTICE 4

PARENT-CHILD SURROGATE

The healing power of touch is well documented, and I use the following exercise on the courses I run because it is one of the most powerful and simple techniques I have found for accelerating healing. FreeMind Peace is all about finding those parts of us that feel afraid and inadequate, and then loving them back to life. So, the following exercise is all about connecting to feelings of being loved, loving, and lovable. That underpins all happiness.

1. Enroll the help of a person who is very comfortable with giving hugs. Tell them this is about you both giving and receiving healing touch in the form of hugs and role-playing loving parents for one another. Let them know the kind of hug you would like and the kind of nurturing touch you would enjoy from a parent. For example, would

you like your face or hair being stroked? You might also want to share a phrase or a sentence that you might like to hear during the experience. For example, 'It's OK now darling. I've got you now,' or 'I am so proud of you. There is nothing you need to do. I love you exactly as you are.'

2. Before you begin, take a few minutes to relax and get very present. Make eye contact, if you're both comfortable with it. As you both breathe, imagine that you are already connecting and softening with each other.

3. Ask them to hold you like a loving parent would hold a child, and allow yourself to surrender into their care. Ensure that both of you are completely comfortable and relaxed. Deepen your breathing and focus on the feeling of melting into one another. Then the parent can slowly stroke your arm or your face, depending on what you discussed, and they can say the words that you asked for. People playing the parent can follow their intuition too by sharing the words they feel compelled to say. At any time, if you want the hug, the stroking, or the words to be different or stopped altogether, just ask for what you want.

4. Choose to feel the embrace exactly the same way a child would enjoy being held by a parent who cherished them. For the person playing the parent, it makes the process more powerful if they focus on connecting to their powerfully loving parental feelings. It can be useful to deeply imagine that the person in their arms is their child. It can also be really powerful and very healing for the person playing the parent to imagine that the person in their arms is their younger self.

5. Then when you feel ready, or the previously agreed amount of time has passed, swap roles. Breathe deeply and open your heart to that being and adore them, stroke their hair, and let them feel utterly adored by you. Let them (yourself) feel that everything is now OK. Everything is safe.

6. After this exercise, take some time to gently discuss your experiences.

FREEMIND PEACE PRACTICE 5

DECLUTTER YOUR LIFE

Take some time to organize and declutter an area of your home or office. Surprisingly, this very practical task can also help you declutter emotionally too. This could be as big as going through your whole house, getting rid of anything that you haven't used or worn in the last two years. Or simply organizing one drawer, which is full of miscellaneous things you never or rarely use. It could even be as simple as clearing out and cleaning a shelf in your refrigerator.

Use this exercise as a ritual for your inner mind. When you are in the process of freeing yourself of old and unwanted thoughts, feelings, beliefs, and behaviors it really helps to have a clear-out of your physical space too. You might also want to make changes in your appearance. Changing how you dress or how you wear your hair can also help you identify with new, more empowered, and positive ways of being in the world.

FREEMIND PEACE PRACTICE 6

....

DETOX YOUR LIFE

Do you remember playing a game when you were younger in which you were searching for something and your parent would say 'warmer' when you were getting closer or 'hotter' when you were really close, or if you started to move in the wrong direction they would say 'cooler,' and so on? Our emotions can serve us in exactly the same way. Our emotions can let us know if we are living in the best way and moving in the best direction. However, that beautiful compass only works if our system is clean.

Unresolved emotions get in the way of clarity, but so does a lack of health and fitness. If the body is clogged with toxins, overtired, overweight or unfit, then our internal compass can be totally obscured. We are most likely not able to feel what is actually happening inside. Our deeper intuitive awareness of nuance and subtlety in understanding what is right for us will be lost.

So, one of the best ways to bring peace and clarity to your life is to bring peace and clarity to your body. Get your body clear, lively, and alive. When we are in peak condition, we are connected to our peace and power so much more beautifully. You will shine and sparkle and you will feel confident in knowing what actions will serve you best.

RECOMMENDED RESOURCES

MUSIC

* Arvo Pärt, 'Spiegel Im Spiegel': Beautiful music for relaxation or meditation.
* Handel and Haydn Society Chorus, 'Agnus Dei': The most beautiful music with which to heal old wounds.
* Joby Talbot, 'February: The Arctic Circle': An incredible piece of modern classical music, which is the perfect soundtrack for visualizing powerful healing conversations with yourself and others. Let the music do the talking.
* Jont, 'Teardrops and Pennies': A beautiful song, which describes how, when we go into our pain, we come out on the other side fully in love with life.
* Jont, 'Hurt to Love': Another beautiful song that focuses on the beauty of letting go.

BOOKS

* Andy White, *Going Mad to Stay Sane*: A great explanation of how and why we choose to sabotage ourselves for beautiful reasons.
* *A Course in Miracles*: An incredible book that is all about the miracles that love and forgiveness brings.

FREEMIND RESOURCES

* **Self-sabotage** A brief video explaining why we block our happiness and success and how to change it. For more information, visit www.freemindproject.org/self or scan the QR code overleaf.

* **FreeMind Home Training System** The FreeMind training recordings combine all of the FreeMind Principles and Practices with powerful hypnosis and metaphorically charged bespoke film score music. This home-training system also includes short support and inspirational videos. For more information about the home training system see Further FreeMind Resources, page 253, visit www.freemindproject.org/3pillars or scan the QR code below).

FreeMind Power: Reprogramming

Pillar 1 is all about clearing away the negative beliefs and feelings that might be holding you back, so that you can be at peace with every part of yourself. Once you are able to accept and love yourself, you are ready for the next stage of the process, FreeMind Power, which focuses on harnessing the power of the mind and its capacity to be conditioned.

Your unconscious is a vast storehouse of capability waiting to be given a chance to shine, and so Pillar 2 is all about learning to reprogram yourself with positive and inspiring thoughts, feelings, and beliefs, so that you can unleash your full and glorious potential. This is what I call 'Success Psychology,' and with those powerful and positive beliefs in place, you can then rest in your natural perfection, trusting that you are the perfect person in the perfect place with the perfect skills to do exactly what is called for. This is the second YES of the Triple YES (see page xviii).

This process is all about your beliefs. For example: What do you currently believe about yourself? How are you with work? Love? Money? Health? Remembering names? Getting up in the morning? Mathematical ability? Drawing pictures? Playing musical instruments? How old do you feel?

What you believe and what you expect totally affect how well you perform. Learning how to use Success Psychology to reprogram your mind and bring out the best from yourself is what FreeMind Power is all about. What follows are a number of case studies, experiments, and stories that I hope will show you the power that you have to bring real and lasting change to your life.

TRAINEE HYPNOTHERAPIST IN ACTION

While I was still training to become a hypnotherapist, my friend John asked me to hypnotize him. At the time, he was struggling to look after himself, not exercising, and partying a little too hard. He was angry with himself and very low. Still, though a trainee, I wanted to help but remained a little hesitant about my skills.

I began by getting him to change his breathing pattern so that he became relaxed. Once he was deeply relaxed, I asked John to remember a time when he had looked after himself. He immediately remembered a time when he was at a Taekwondo grading. In this memory he was in peak condition. He felt amazingly fit, vibrant, and powerful. In order to help him connect with those feelings, I encouraged him to make the memory more vivid. I asked him to make the colors in the pictures brighter and the sounds louder; and to remember the feeling of his outfit on his body and his bare feet on the floor.

Once he started to feel very powerfully how good it

is to be fit, healthy, and happy, I asked him to deepen his breathing and then led him to imagine himself three months from now, looking amazing, feeling fit, and happy. I asked him to combine the feelings from the positive memory with his expectations for the future. At this point tears welled up in his eyes. At that peak moment, I asked him to repeat, 'Each and every day, I am loving looking after myself more and more.' Every time he said the phrase, he looked more determined, sounded happier, and clearly was feeling very motivated.

I brought him back out of the relaxation with suggestions that he could give himself the gift of health and happiness every day that he exercised. He opened his eyes and hugged me while thanking me profusely and then left immediately to go for a run. He literally ran away up the beach full of energy. On his return, he was ablaze with vitality and joy, and over the next few months I received various inspirational text messages of thanks and gratitude about his newfound fitness and happiness.

Just 20 minutes of simple reprogramming techniques helped John to change what he thought about himself and how he was behaving, and brought home to me the power of the mind. See FreeMind Power Practice 1 to do this for yourself (page 167).

....

THE PRINCIPLES OF SUCCESS PSYCHOLOGY

By thinking and feeling differently, we are able to live our lives with new beliefs and ideas about who we are and what we do. Using these techniques, you can make changes in your life to create the life that you want. The principles are simple:

* Connect deeply with the thoughts and feelings associated with being the kind of person that you want to be.
* Believe you are that person in potential and that you are becoming that person more and more every day.
* Repeat to yourself some of the vision statements (see page 171) that support these empowered ways of thinking, feeling, and being.
* Remember that your greatest potential has always been inside you. It is simply waiting for you to align with it.
* Be your potential now by choosing and prioritizing new behaviors that are aligned with you being your best.

....

AGING IS ALL IN THE MIND

Ellen Langer, from Harvard, conducted one of my favorite studies on mind reprogramming in 1979, described in her brilliant book *Counter Clockwise*, which demonstrates the power of belief. A group of men aged 75 were taken to a ranch and asked to pretend that they were 20 years younger. The ranch was freshly decorated in a fashion in keeping with 20 years earlier; old TV shows were piped in, old newspapers were reprinted, and the men encouraged to speak about their old jobs and their families, in ways which all supported the notion that they were 20 years younger.

During that time many amazing things occurred but one of the most compelling findings were the 'before' and 'after' photographs that were taken of these men. A panel of objective judges thought the men looked considerably younger in the 'after' photos. In addition, a system of medical age markers (that is, blood pressure, cholesterol, energy levels, strength, posture, perception, cognition, memory, and many more advanced tests) was used to assess the levels of aging of the men before and after. After only one week, most of the men showed some reversals of the aging process, some of which could be described as rapid reversals.

....

In this extraordinary piece of research, the following maxim becomes clear: What we focus on, what we believe, the words we use, and the way we live condition us to experience ourselves and the world in a certain way. Reprogramming involves using that feature of the human mind and taking responsibility for our own conditioning. By learning how to build empowering beliefs we can radically affect what we perceive, how we feel, and how we perform. Otherwise our world is a reflection of our unconscious and potentially limiting beliefs and that can cloud everything, as the following story demonstrates.

....

OUR BELIEFS CREATE OUR REALITY

A wise old man is sitting on an old bench just outside of his village when a traveler approaches him. The traveler tells him that he is weary of traveling and looking for a nice place to settle down. The traveler asks the old man what the people are like in his village. The old man replies by asking the traveler what the people were like where he has come from. The traveler explains that in the last village he visited, people were mean, negative, unhelpful, untrustworthy, and generally unpleasant. The old man sighs and says that the traveler would find most of the people in this village much the same. The traveler lowers his eyes and decides to continue his search elsewhere.

The next day the old man is sitting there again and another traveler approaches him and asks him the same question. Once again, the old man asks him what the people were like where he has come from. The traveler explains that people were generally lovely, positive, helpful, trustworthy, and pleasant. The old man smiles widely, welcomes the man into the village and explains that he would find most of the people in this village much the same.

....

We find what we expect because what we see is a projection of who we are and what we believe.

THE PRINCIPLES OF REPROGRAMMING

The brain constantly filters reality and only lets us become consciously aware of things that fit our model of the world. For instance, you are not consciously aware of all the information that is coming to your mind at the moment. While you have been reading, it hasn't been relevant so your inner mind hasn't bothered to let you be conscious of it. And that might be a car going by outside, the washing machine rumbling away in the background, or the feeling of your toes in this moment. That data (sensory feelings) has been arriving in your brain this whole time but it has been filtered out. So, it's worth considering what other aspects of yourself might currently be out of your conscious awareness. Maybe you have the capacity to be an even more amazing lover, an incredible snowboarder, a multi-linguist, a storyteller, or an inspirational speaker? Reprogramming works by drawing your attention to previously unrecognized potential.

Humans have on average 60,000 thoughts a day and most of those thoughts are the same thoughts we had the day before. We have a habit of programming ourselves every day. For example, we might tell ourselves that we can't sing, we are no good at directions, or can't cope without a certain amount of sleep every night. We might have unnecessarily fixed ideas about how good we are at speaking in public, parking cars, or relationships. Reprogramming involves us connecting to more belief in our abilities.

SELF-FULFILLING BELIEFS

Two psychologists, Rosenthal and Jacobson,[5] demonstrated this innate human ability in the late 1960s when they took a classroom of young children and tested their levels of intelligence and effectiveness at school. As the children were young, they predominantly had one teacher for most of their lessons. Rosenthal and Jacobson then told the teacher the names of three of the children who were intelligent and destined to do well. The children were not informed that they had been selected.

In truth, the three children were actually from the average section of the class, and were not especially intelligent at all. However, by the end of the year, those children had done much better than their counterparts. What the psychologists were studying was the attitude of the teacher toward them. What they discovered was the teacher operated with a kind of implied expectation. When any of those three children struggled, the teacher dealt with them in a way in which those children felt that the teacher really believed in them. That belief was contagious and they began to believe in themselves more and so they thrived.

....

Of course, the results of Rosenthal and Jacobson's experiment make total sense and are not that surprising, but vital information if you are a teacher, or a parent, or a manager. However, it is also important to consider how these principles play out inside your mind. When you run into difficulty do you meet yourself with total belief? Do you think of yourself as gifted, intelligent, and able to cope? What implied expectations do you have about yourself? FreeMind reprogramming is all about putting you in the most positive and powerful state of mind so that you can bring out the best performance from yourself. When every part of us believes in a new possibility, the unconscious has the power to make it manifest. This is really the essence of faith.

....

THE POWER OF TRUTH, CONGRUENCE, AND INTEGRITY

In another famous story, Mahatma Gandhi was once approached by a woman who had walked for days to meet him. She was desperate for him to speak to her son to get him to stop eating sugary cakes and candies. Like the rest of India, her son was a huge fan of Gandhi, and she hoped he would have the power to make an impression upon her son and get him to change his ways.

Gandhi heard her concerns and asked her to bring her son to see him again in a month's time. She was both pleased and a little frustrated. She had come a long way and had to wait a very long time to get an audience. Sure enough, though, she and her son went home and a month later returned and waited to see him again. Upon seeing her, Gandhi remembered her immediately and asked her to bring her son in. At that point he made himself tall, he very sternly placed both hands on the boy's shoulders, and he loomed over him and commanded with everything that he could muster, 'STOP EATING SUGAR.'

The boy was shaken to his core and, vibrating with certainty, pledged that he would do as he was told. He left the room, but his mother remained. She was both pleased and a little confused – and, dare I say, a bit annoyed. 'Why,' she enquired, 'didn't you do that last time?' Gandhi simply replied, 'A month ago, I was eating sugar.'

....

When every part of you is aligned with the truth – when you are certain of what you are saying and its importance, and when that message is conveyed with love – you will have the power to move mountains. This is why it is so important to live with integrity. Ideally our life is a beautiful reflection of our most inspiring ideals. Gandhi said, 'Freedom comes when everything you think, say, and do are in alignment.' Saying what we mean and meaning what we say, sticking to our agreements, being honest in all of our dealings, and being proud of who we are and how we do things are vital for living with fully embodied congruence. When you are absolutely 'walking your talk,' you start to connect to a tremendous amount of power.

It is impossible to believe in ourselves, love ourselves, and experience total confidence-filled faith if we are harboring resentments, anger, negativity, and so on. That is why the deprogramming and release work is so important, but once it is done, we can use new language patterns, we can create new images in our mind, we can expect people to respond to us more powerfully, and we can start to see ourselves in a much more empowered way. When we can operate with that level of trust (faith) truly amazing things can happen.

This is not about becoming a different person. This is about you reclaiming your true power. This is about you experiencing who you would have been had you always received the perfect love and support when you were growing up. This is about rediscovering who you would have been had you never experienced any NO states. If, in every moment of your life, you felt safe, protected, valued, nurtured, respected, inspired, and honored you would most likely find it so much easier to love and be loved; so much easier to create and contribute; so much easier to enjoy life to the full. In that place we flow with a brilliance that shines with an especially beautiful glow. We feel it, and everyone else can sense it too.

EMBODYING THE DIVINE

In old Bedouin Islamic tribes, dancing used to be a huge part of the community. They would set up camp and after the evening meal they would play music and dance. It was understood in those times that every now and again a dancer would become enraptured by the divine. To all who were there, a sort of possession became visible. The dancer, overtaken by inspiration, would move in such a way that the evidence of the divine moving through them was obvious. They became graceful, powerful, and expressive in especially provocative ways. When this happened, the people watching would start chanting over and over again, 'Allah, Allah, Allah,' and the dancer would dance like never before. Through invasion and migration this culture and practice spread into other countries. Evidence of this ancient appreciation of the 'divine performance' is still visible in Spain today. When a flamenco dancer begins to shine and dance especially well, the onlookers still shout out the Spanish word 'Olé' at peak moments, which thousands of years ago was the word 'Allah.'

That feeling of crying out with joy for having seen or been touched by a divine performance is actually very common. Many of us have seen it before. In fact, most of the joy of watching soccer is about moments of gold, in an otherwise continuously difficult and almost mundane struggle to make something happen. Teams battle against each other to make something work. The pass falls short or the shot goes wide.

But suddenly, out of nowhere, something magical happens. A pass is pitched perfectly and lands sweetly at the feet of a player who appears in the perfect place, they turn and beat one defender, and there is a lightness and brightness to them that captures everyone's hope. The spectators rise to their feet. The player turns and beats another player, the people watching stop breathing. Instead of going for personal glory, the player passes the ball to his teammate who, with one glorious kick, slams the ball into the back of the net. The goalkeeper never had a chance. The crowd goes mad, cheering their own (although often lewd) divine chant. In that moment, pure magic happens. Everything is coordinated; everything works. It has a divine rhythm and everything makes sense – the purest art that makes the entire struggle worthwhile.

You may have also heard about the famous 20-minute standing ovation in honor of Rudolf Nureyev, arguably the best male ballet dancer the world has ever known. In this one performance, something happened during one of his leaps that has entered dancing legend. He flew up from the ground with such force that the crowd gasped as he seemed to hang in the air, but somehow, with their gasp, he expanded himself further and appeared to lift even higher into the air and be suspended for an extra moment longer. Those who saw it experienced something of the divine that night.

Somewhere between the powers we have to move beyond limitation, and the capacity we have to bring out from ourselves more artful ways of doing things, we can truly touch the very heart of what it is to be alive, free, and wonderful. This is also what the world's wisdom and spiritual traditions have been trying to tell us. Wanting us to know that beyond our resentments and our ideas about what is possible, there is a place of beauty and grandeur waiting to be experienced, where in full flow and harmony we can be the vessel for the most extraordinary of performances.

Discovering that artful power is the hero's journey. This is Luke Skywalker putting away his aiming equipment and trusting the 'force.' While this can at times be the perfect leap in ballet or the most poetic of goals, it can also be a loving piece of parenting, an elegant piece of parking, or even a simple choice to see the good in a situation that, at first glance, may appear to be bad. Making our lives into an art form is not a 'should' or a 'must.' It is simply an opportunity to discover for ourselves what it means to live with faith and grace in every moment. This is the realization of freedom. This is reprogramming at its best.

When we are truly free in the moment we are fully present.

In these 'flow' states we are not really thinking about what we are doing or how we are doing it. We are both lost and found in the immediate action. It is more of an unveiling than it is a creation. It is not about doing your best. It is simply about being your best.

There is another amazing story about Laurence Olivier's extraordinary performance of *Hamlet* one night. Something special happened. The crowd witnessed something that made them feel some divine stirring and gave him a standing ovation. That is why these moments are so powerful for us. We love our full potential to be represented by a performer who is fully artful (graceful/blessed). Well, on this night

Olivier had outdone himself, and yet a friend of his was very surprised to find Olivier in his dressing room in a foul mood. His friend remarked, 'Why are you so upset. That was the performance of your life. Never have I seen Hamlet performed like that!' Olivier, in total exasperation and frustration, shouted: 'DON'T YOU THINK I KNOW THAT!' 'Well' enquired the friend further, 'what's the problem?' To which Olivier shouted, 'I DON'T KNOW IF I WILL EVER BE ABLE TO DO IT AGAIN!'

PRAYER IS A REPROGRAMMING TECHNIQUE

Reprogramming is about developing beliefs and behaviors that are consistent with extraordinary performances. It is not about making something happen out of nothing, but rather getting out of the way of our selves and allowing the divine brilliance to flow through. It has been said that an amateur practices until they can do something but a professional practices until they can't fail to do something. Reprogramming is about trusting in the infinite intelligence of your unconscious. That is the source of your greatest potential and your belief in that power makes up the bedrock of your faith in life. So, the FreeMind Power Practices (see page 165) are about reprogramming yourself to create an ultimate state of belief or faith.

The key to reprogramming is to experience yourself as though you already have the trait, feeling, skill, or change in place. Nothing but your perception needs to change. All of our challenges come from the idea that we are inadequate and that something needs to be different. If instead we can rest in our innate perfection and trust that all will be well, we can operate with a deeply solid faith in ourselves and the universe as a whole. That kind of faith has immense power.

The stories and events that most inspire us – such as Nureyev's or Olivier's, for example – all point to the same truth. They hint at the same extraordinary capacity lying dormant in all of us that is waiting to be unleashed. That ache for perfect self-expression, that desire for greatness, that liberation from fear and remembrance of our true unlimited nature – that is the purpose of reprogramming.

When I studied the ancient spiritual texts and philosophies, the concept of prayer kept returning. I realized pretty soon that the kind of prayer being described was more a matter of developing a practice to deepen your faith. In my ignorance, I had thought prayer was all about talking to some form of a separate God. Now, I realize that many prayer processes are actually about alignment with the divine power that already exists inside us. This is less about getting something and more about being something. Prayer began to resemble what I was learning about reprogramming.

The prayer, or reprogramming, that works best is not an act of begging. This isn't a process of supplication where we are small and separate from the greatness. This isn't coming from one needy person over here and going out to something generous and divine 'over there.' It is simply an act of alignment with your ultimate potential, where you can reconnect to a greater sense of awareness that you are all things already.

In this moment you are the perfect expression of greatness. You are directly connected to everything you ever needed. It is with you now, but no matter how much you want to make the sun rise in the West or no matter how much you pray for the tide to stop, you will not make that happen. You are all-powerful but your will cannot alter the course of your nature. Prayer or reprogramming is not about manifestation, creation, or even control. When it works best it is about empowered alignment and surrender.

There are many modern-day spiritual teachers who promote the overly simple and dangerous idea that you can use reprogramming techniques to change external reality. They say, for example, we can attract desirable things to us by vividly visualizing them. If it were that simple, 14-year-old boys would be waking up next to porn stars every morning. Reprogramming is simply about clearing away the blocks in our perceptions that previously hid our true nature from us.

Michelangelo was once asked about how he carved the glorious statue of *David* from a notoriously difficult piece of rock. He simply answered, 'David was already in the rock. All I had to do was simply remove everything that wasn't him.' In so many ways we are large hulking blocks of marble that think of ourselves as monosyllabic rectangles of rock. When we align ourselves with who we really are on the inside, that which isn't true falls away and our true glory is revealed. This is prayer at its most natural. Not a creation but rather a revelation. This is reprogramming at its best. When we are at peace and in love with ourselves as we are, we become infinitely more powerful and effective. With that energy we bless our lives and, yes, we are then much more likely to get all the things we ever wanted.

This is FreeMind Power, and when you are operating with that confidence, congruence, and charisma it is much more likely that you will have more fun, make more money, have more enjoyable relationships, and so on. So if you pray for anything, let it simply be for remembrance of that which you already are. Let it be a prayer of gratitude for the joy you already have, and the riches you already own. Gratitude is the most creative force in the universe, as this next story demonstrates.

....

THE KENTISH TOWN MIRACLE

Some years ago I was stuck in London's Kentish Town subway station because the rain was so heavy that had I walked out in it I would have been soaked through in seconds. The rain was annoying but I was already irritated because I was on my way to pay for an unexpected repair on my car. I was frustrated because I couldn't afford the repair and definitely couldn't afford the time required to drop off and pick up the car from the garage. I needed to collect the car before they closed at 5pm and only had 20 minutes to get there but I really didn't want to get wet.

I needed the car so that I could go to a party that night and was already dressed in the clothes that I planned to wear, so I really didn't want to get soaked. I looked at the torrential rain and couldn't help feeling pretty sorry for myself. To my mind everything was wrong and I was thoroughly fed up. I knew my mindset was making the whole situation worse, so I decided to stop counting my grievances and start counting my blessings. I moved from a NO to a YES. I realized that I was lucky that the steering hadn't dangerously failed on a busy road. I also appreciated that there was a garage that specialized in my make of car nearby, which meant I managed to avoid the expense of getting it towed. Plus, the garage had availability to work on the car.

Pretty soon I started to feel much better. I was reprogramming my perception and as I did that I couldn't help feeling that somehow the rain situation was going to be OK too. I started to feel blessed and pledged that, no matter what, at 4.50pm, I would walk out of the subway station with my head held high in faith. I secretly hoped the rain would stop but I decided to trust that all would be well no matter what.

However, instead of subsiding the rain started pounding even harder; nevertheless, it was time to go, so I marched toward the exit. However, just as I got there, I totally recoiled from walking out into the downpour. In that nanosecond I was harsh with myself for not following through and being afraid. But because I had been moving at such speed and then slowed so suddenly (almost to a stop but not quite), my right arm swung up in front of me. At that EXACT moment, a person arrived at the station holding an umbrella aloft. It had been battered and broken by the heavy downpour but still worked. 'Does anyone want this?' he said and at that precise moment I emerged from the exit, with my arm swinging so high that, miraculously, it was less than two inches from the umbrella being offered to me. His offer had barely been uttered before I had it in my hands and was off down the street shouting, 'Thank you' over my shoulder.

REPROGRAMMING FAITH
INCLUDES LOVING OUR FEAR
AND TRUSTING THE TIMING

The thing that I find most powerful about that experience is not the magic of having received the umbrella. It is rather how my anxiety, doubt, and fear made the timing perfect. Had I not recoiled in the final moment I would have shot past him and someone else would have been nearer. I was so quick to hate myself for not having more faith, for not trusting more, for not being more ready to go out into the wet. But it was exactly that fear which put my hand in the perfect place at the perfect time.

If the universe is perfect, anxiety must have its place too. Everything has a season. Everything has timing. Seeds have growth inhibitors in them that prevent them from sprouting until they are ready. In spring the seeds get wet, and the enzyme-blocking growth-inhibitors dissolve away and the plants start to grow again. Anxiety, doubt, and resistance are all part of the perfect unfolding. Going from NO to YES is a seasonal thing. Sometimes we are in contraction and at other times we are in bloom. What never ceases to amaze me are the blessings that we fail to appreciate on a daily basis and the miracles that we therefore never create. Our acceptance or better celebration of 'what is' is the ultimate collaboration. With that primary YES in place, a whole new dance becomes possible.

Most of us have experienced one of those moments where we feel something happened because it was supposed to, although we have dismissed it as coincidence or sheer good luck. Have you? Have you ever felt something had a special significance? Like it was destined or in alignment with something being called for. The YES state feels very differently to the NO state. The YES state is light, open, collaborative, and creative. In the YES state you can meet the present moment and magic can happen. The NO state is contracted, disconnected, confused, cold, and complicated. Nothing works in that place and nothing feels good. Can you feel the difference between those days when you are in alignment and everything is flowing compared to those days where everything is complicated and disjointed?

The YES state is the feeling of faith. From there things fall into place in such a way that it feels obvious that the universe is unfolding in the perfect way at the perfect time. Those moments of synchronicity or alignment can be hugely useful in helping us relax into the flow of life.

The universe simply cannot be a divinely ordered and perfect place at times and not at other times.

It either is or it isn't. It simply can't be both. It is either on or off. Therefore, if you have ever had one of those numinous magical moments of synchronicity, connection, or oneness, then you can rest assured. It is on. Everything is part of that 'on-ness,' or oneness, and therefore nothing is ever wrong.

BEING A PART OF THE ONENESS

At some point, we have to decide whether the world is OK or it isn't OK. Personally, I have seen enough evidence in my life and the lives of my clients to assure me that the universe is unfolding in the perfect way at the perfect time. Even the suffering is perfect because it always comes from fear and resistance. All of your upsets and difficulties can be seen as invitations for you to come back to that perspective of faith, to return to love, to come back to YES, and to come back home.

When we are in our state of YES, we are usually filled with enthusiasm; and this lively energy is highly contagious. The word 'enthusiasm' means to be filled with god (*en-theos* means 'god within'). The word 'inspiration' means to be filled with spirit or life energy. It shares the same Latin root *spire* (meaning 'life force' or 'energy') with the words spirituality and respiration. When we are aligned with this divine energy we are delightful. That word means we are literally 'coming' or 'filled with' light. You know how amazing that feels. It seems to me that life is an opportunity to overcome difficulties by remembering that the greatest joy can be found in being our most amazing and empowered self. Can you feel that ancient yearning inside yourself?

Our inner being is constantly seeking more beautiful expressions of itself. I don't believe in a separate bearded-style God but I do believe that our inner mind or soul is ever-ready to lead us toward ways of being that are more naturally, loving and wise. This is the best way to be successful and happy. Underneath all of our resistance, competitiveness, and fear there is a heart that beats with a deep wisdom of the interconnected nature of life. Even if you don't buy into this idea of a single field of consciousness (which I'll discuss in more detail in Pillar 3, see page 183), wisdom suggests that being loving and seeing all things as connected and interdependent is sensible. A very wise Roman emperor, Marcus Aurelius, pointed this logic out almost 2,000 years ago when he said, 'Rational beings exist for one another. That which is not good for the swarm, neither is it good for the bee.'

HUMANS ARE MEANING-MAKING MACHINES

If you look hard enough around you it's possible to feel your mind, body, and soul begging you to learn from the patterns around you and return to a more harmonious way of being. For instance, right now you could choose to randomly open this or any other book at any page and select a random paragraph. You could read that paragraph and interpret it to be a key message of guidance for you at this stage of your life. What could you choose to make that mean? How might you be able to interpret that message, so as to glean some wisdom to improve your life?[6] Try that now.

Don't be disheartened if you didn't get anything. I am just trying to highlight the power we have to create valuable meaning. The fact that we make up the meaning doesn't make that meaning any less real. I saw a TV show by Derren Brown[7] once in which a woman was tricked into thinking that for the next two weeks paid actors would be interacting with her in her normal everyday life. She was told these seemingly random strangers would be creating life lessons for her to get more out of her life. In truth, there were no actors but, sure enough, after two weeks she had interpreted totally random interactions and had made them mean something. She had decided to spend more time with her loved ones and to live her life in greater balance. She was already putting those plans into practice.

The TV show did this experiment to highlight that people with religious beliefs interpret the random experiences of life in a way that fits their beliefs. The show was trying to demonstrate that people imagine that God is communicating with them. However, perhaps the show missed the point. If it had repeated that experiment with thousands of people, the results would have been the same. No surprise there, but what else would have been similar? That is the important question. The messages and interpretations would all have been along exactly the same lines. They would have followed themes of those people being more open, loving, engaged, happier, more balanced, more fulfilled, more connected, more alive, etc. That is what your unconscious wants for you.

There is a benevolent driving force in the world. It is your inner mind, your unconscious, or your soul if you prefer that term. That wiser part of you is continuously trying to help you live in more beautiful and balanced ways. That is the spiritual journey and all we have to do is to take the time to listen. To let our souls guide us to a sweeter more loving life. This show didn't disprove God to me. It completely confirmed my understanding of spirituality and my appreciation of the human heart and its inherent desire for happiness.

If you decide that life is a divine unfolding where you are being guided to live a full and happy life, your world will become more beautiful every single day.

I know that I choose to relate to my life in this way, and I know that I am then fitting my experiences into that model. It helps me to be happy. For me, I don't mind what you do or don't believe in. I am only interested in the degree to which what you believe in enables you to be more peaceful, positive, and loving with yourself and others. That is ideally what the religious or spiritual journey is all about. The metaphor you use to inspire you to do that is your business.

EVERYTHING IS AN OPPORTUNITY IF YOU BELIEVE IT TO BE

I choose to see everything as a representation of where we are in our lives: Every relationship and every interaction is a reflection of the peace and love we are operating with. If we are experiencing conflict then we must internally be set against ourselves. Everything is an opportunity for us to see how we could be more free and happy. Everything then, including our darkest moments, is an opportunity to feel the touch of the divine inviting us home. With this metaphor (which could also be called a philosophy or outlook) the magic, beauty, and interconnectedness of everything is tangible in every moment.

Perhaps everything is random and I'm just deluding myself. I can't guarantee that that isn't the case, but I can give a 100-percent guarantee that magical things happen when you view the world with this perspective. I can guarantee that if you choose to see the world through that filter you will be happier, more confident, more alive, and more willing to take more beautiful and courageous actions for yourself and others. Imagine for a moment how that might improve your life?

So, let's say all of this is just an imaginary delusion. Does it actually matter if, by believing that, you think, feel, and behave in more amazing ways, and it makes you more effective, more powerful, and more secure? Every time I help my clients experience the sensation of faith and gratitude flowing from feeling part of a unified field of loving intelligence their lives get infinitely better. Other people start trusting them more, other people want to invest in them, their relationships are more alive, and their work is more successful and lucrative. Time and time again this confirms and refreshes my prayer for remembrance of this simple fact:

Coming from peace and love is the best way to bless your life.

FREEMIND METAPHORICAL PROGRAMMING

Understanding how we 'make meaning' led me to look more deeply at the mechanics of metaphor. Metaphors can be incredibly powerful because they can bypass the conscious mind (where our limited beliefs block our ability to be happy) and deliver meaning and instructions directly to the unconscious mind. For example, a great story can inspire us to be more open and loving. A great analogy can make a complicated concept much more comprehensible. A metaphorical story, packed full of symbolic meaning, can powerfully impart wisdom and inspire positive action.

MUSIC AS METAPHOR

In the early years of my work, I spent a lot of time helping clients reprogram their beliefs. While they were hypnotized, I used metaphorical stories, constructed vivid visualizations, and designed empowered language patterns for them. This preparation was in the hope of directing them to feel more confident and able. However, as my work progressed, I discovered that it is actually a lot more powerful to direct the process less and trust the innate healing capacity of the client's unconscious more. The most effective way I found to make that process work was using music.

I started inviting my clients to listen to a piece of music as the sound of their unconscious beliefs changing. I made the music a metaphor. So, now when I work with clients who want to speak to a part of their mind that is holding them back, I use hypnosis to get them relaxed. I then invite them to visualize that part of themselves that is responsible for self-sabotage (for example, anxiety, smoking, overeating, anger, and so on). Then instead of directing that healing conversation or negotiating on their behalf, I simply say the following piece of music is the sound of you resolving this challenge. Take the time to understand what needs to be understood and allow each note of the music to be the thoughts and feelings that need to be thought and felt. I also invite them to allow the music to inspire them to make whatever internal agreements and decisions are needed to bring themselves into alignment with more effective and happier ways of living. I then simply play a beautiful piece of music and let their unconscious interpret that music in ways that enable them to heal themselves.

It constantly amazes me how brilliant the unconscious mind is when it is given clear instructions and a powerful metaphor. After these sessions my clients describe how the music became the soundtrack to the most extraordinary resolution. People find themselves saying the perfect thing in the perfect way. Their minds come up with the perfect solutions to their problems and their visualizations are infinitely more creative than anything I could construct. Using music and hypnotherapy in this way is like inducing a waking dream state.

. . . .

Try using these music and relaxation reprogramming techniques yourself and you might be amazed at how your mind pictures different parts of yourself. Aspects of your being might be represented as a ball of light, or you may find a kind of sergeant major in your consciousness all too ready to tear a strip off you. You may see your heart as defended with a wall around it or you might see a version of yourself in the future full of light and power. Sometimes my clients don't report anything visual at all but describe feelings of deep resistance being dissolved. Each note of the music becomes the most eloquent healing intervention working on the deepest part of the inner mind. When you can set a clear intention and allow yourself to be led by a beautiful piece of music your inner mind will know exactly what to do to help you live with more peace, power, and purpose.

However, you don't have to rely just on music. We can ascribe meaning to everything that we do. This is about creating living rituals by bringing consciousness and intention to our every action to create change. You could wash the dishes as a ritualized metaphorical act of opening to gratitude. You could do your tax forms or pay your bills as an exercise to remind you of the principles of generosity. You could go for a winter walk in nature and invite yourself to use it as a way to come to terms with the idea of change, and even death, being an intrinsic part of life. You could choose to listen to a beautiful piece of music as the sound of yourself truly accepting and loving yourself. Your heart-mind is waiting to help you free yourself in any and every moment.

The more I work with the unconscious the more I realize how it is just waiting to help us find ways to more beautiful expressions of our possibility. Whether you believe in God or not, there is a universal benevolent loving force that can bring great joy and abundance to your life and it speaks to you in the heart of your inner mind. Just to read these words your unconscious has to process millions of bits of information every second. Your unconscious is currently running your immune system, regulating your digestion, and taking care of the coordination of 60 trillion cells working in harmony to keep you alive in this moment.

Your unconscious is a genius. The human conscious mind can, on average, manage to think about a maximum of nine things at any one time. It is most likely, then, that your inner mind has a better idea of what will serve you, and it is steering you toward that every day. When we can reclaim our direct connection to our unconscious and trust that it is far more powerful than we could ever imagine, we can relax back into an unfolding evolution that, if we are paying attention, will give us many signs to enable us to find our own way to freedom and happiness.

REPROGRAMMING YOURSELF
BY CHALLENGING YOUR FEARS

Making a practice of lovingly pushing yourself to confront your fears and developing your courage is the best way to bring more happiness to your life. Our desire to be safe and comfortable is understandable, but unfortunately those conservative energies can hold in place all sorts of limiting ideas and beliefs we have about ourselves. By choosing to do things that you wouldn't usually do – which might be public speaking, bungee jumping, mountain climbing, or simply trying a new food or making conversation with a stranger – you automatically change your programming.

Being bold and trying new things naturally evolves your identity because it widens your idea of yourself, deepens your love for yourself, and connects you with a life force that can light up the world. What is more, it is incredibly exciting and invigorating to do something that you were once too afraid to do. Making a commitment to stretch yourself is a vital part of bringing your best to life. Your comfort zone holds in place everything that is holding you back. This practice is probably one of the most powerful life-changing tools in the world. You are more capable than you can possibly imagine. If your ultimate potential could speak to you, who would it ask you to enjoy being today?

THE MOST POWERFUL MOTIVATOR FOR CHANGE IS LOVE

If you were asked to walk barefoot across hot coals or broken glass you might hesitate before venturing forward. If, however, you had to do this immediately to save the life of a loved one, you wouldn't pause for a moment. Love is the greatest motivator. The word courage comes from the French word for heart (*coeur*). The word literally means 'to come from the heart.' Courage, therefore, is not the absence of fear but the willingness to act even though the fear is there.

FreeMind Power is about developing a deeply loving relationship with yourself and your potential. It is about being excited to stretch yourself because of the love you have for the possibility that you are. It is about loving yourself so much that you want to confront and overcome your fears. It is about not allowing your self to be held back by limitation and resistance. Challenging yourself to develop your courage enables you to be your most amazing, energized, and vibrant self.

FreeMind Power Practices

What follows are a number of different exercises and practices that you can start to experiment with, to help you bring more power into your life. This process is about unleashing the potential that is already there, not about adding something to you that is lacking. This is about learning how to engage with your unconscious mind to connect to an extraordinary source of intelligence and capability. To relax into the flow of your natural brilliance and let yourself shine with greatness.

FreeMind Power is all about confidence, congruence, creativity, and charisma. These are the cornerstones of all great leadership, and with these practices you will be able to bring out the very best from yourself and others.

At the end of this section there is also a list of recommended resources that can support you in becoming more powerful (see page 180).

....

USING THE FREEMIND PRACTICES

When using the inner FreeMind Practices, it is important that you make yourself comfortable before you start – for example, ensure that you won't be disturbed, and allow plenty of time to do the process completely. When doing these exercises it is normal for your mind to wander and it is fine for you to move around to keep yourself comfortable. If possible:

* Do the exercises with your eyes comfortably closed.
* Allow yourself to become very still (your ability to do that will improve over time).
* Just take note of what you notice. You may find that some parts of the exercise are easier than others, but these are not things that you can get wrong.
* Don't get frustrated with yourself or think that these experiences have to be anything in particular.
* Keep an open mind. It is normal to have doubts.
* Give each exercise at least two good attempts. You may also notice that, at times, certain exercises won't work at all for you. In this case, try a different exercise or repeat it at a later time and you may respond differently.

As you allow yourself to go on these inner FreeMind journeys more and more, you may notice strange sensations, such as heaviness or lightness, in your body. You may even feel as if you are going numb. These are all perfectly normal reactions. You can stop whenever you want and your body will rapidly return to its usual sensations.

Wherever possible, become curious about the physical effects of the exercises. They are usually very positive signs that you have become deeply relaxed, which has been proven to be very good for both mind and body.

Some of the practices may take some getting used to but feel free to make them work for you. Be patient, generous, and collaborative. Don't hope they will 'do' something to you. Work with them to help them help you.

....

FREEMIND POWER PRACTICE 1

POWER PROCESS

If you are going to reprogram your mind to enjoy your life fully, it works best when you are relaxed. What follows is a set of different tips and ideas that you can practice and develop to help you to relax more easily and more rapidly. When you are relaxed you can reprogram your mind much more easily, which leads you to naturally change the way you do things. Living your life from a relaxed place is the key to operating with power.

Read the guidelines first but, whenever you can, find a way to make these tools your own. You might want to enlist the help of a friend who can read the guidelines to you so you don't need to remember anything. Each of the steps can be practiced separately but when they are combined they will allow you to connect with amazing amounts of power.

If you choose to practice the steps separately then bring the experience to a close by allowing your attention to come back to your body. Wiggle your fingers and toes and gently open your eyes.

1. Get in a comfortable position, either sitting up or lying down, then focus on slowing your breathing down. Exhale all the air out of your body and gently pause at the bottom of each breath before inhaling the next. Most people don't let go of all of the air so concentrate on gently letting go of all of the air in your body, flattening your belly toward your spine. Then, when you breathe in, inhale slowly and fully. When your lungs are full, gently pause before breathing out. Do this exercise very gently and comfortably, making each breath last for as long as possible.

2. Consciously choose to relax every part of your body. You may want to start at your feet or head, and then simply breathe out from those places, giving them permission to relax. Allow each part in turn to feel valued and thank them for all that they do for you. Concentrate on holding positive feelings for each part of your body, making sure you include your head.

3. Once relaxed, picture yourself in a place of great natural beauty (this releases dopamine into the system, which relaxes us further). It could be somewhere you know well, such as a vacation destination, or maybe a fantasy island, or an imaginary woodland paradise. Allow it to be a place that feels good and happy. Think of the colors, the sounds, the tastes, the smells, and the textures that you would experience there. Change your clothes in your mind and be there as vividly as possible in your imagination. At the same time, allow a feeling of relaxation and gratitude to pour through you. Center yourself in the experience and enjoy it as much as possible.

4. Bring the experience to a close by allowing your attention to come back to your body. Wiggle your fingers and toes and gently open your eyes.

You can enjoy going to this relaxing and peaceful place whenever you are feeling stressed or upset, and you might find it helpful in finding your peaceful and powerful center. However, you might also choose to go to any number of different memories that may help you to be more effective in life. For example, before doing a presentation you might want to spend time vividly enjoying a memory of a time when you did something really well. Or you could remember a time when you were very funny and entertaining. You might like to spend time reconnecting to the early days of your relationship to reinvigorate the love you feel for your partner. You might want to remember a time when you felt especially fit and attractive. These can all be very powerful ways to reprogram yourself and bring any number of different capabilities to life.

FREEMIND POWER PRACTICE 2

DEEPER RELAXATION

The more relaxed you get, the more powerful your reprogramming sessions can be. Regularly experiencing deep relaxation is one of the best methods of achieving what you want from life. This following practice is one of the most popular techniques for inducing deep levels of relaxation, and involves using a scale of descending numbers to deepen an existing level of relaxation.

1. Use steps 1 and 2 of FreeMind Power Practice 1 (above) to help you to become relaxed.
2. Tell yourself that you are about to count down from ten to one.
3. Tell yourself that with each descending number you will go one-tenth deeper into relaxation.
4. Tell yourself that by the number five you will be halfway down and really enjoying it.
5. Tell yourself (and believe) that once you get to the number one, you will be very deeply relaxed.
6. Take a moment to imagine being deeply relaxed with each number.
7. Take a moment to imagine being completely relaxed by the time you have counted down to the number one.
8. Induce the feeling of being deeply relaxed and expect each number to relax you.
9. At the next out breath, breathe gently expelling all the air and right at the end of the breath silently count the number ten.
10. Take two more long, slow breaths and at the end of the second out breath, count down to the next number.
11. Continue counting down at the end of each second out breath.
12. Each time you say the number, pause to feel its effects, and feel everything slowing down and becoming more peaceful.
13. With each descending number, tell yourself that you are going even deeper into relaxation.
14. Notice that during the second half of the countdown how your body feels much more relaxed.

15. At the count of number one, notice the very deep level of relaxation flowing through your mind and body.

16. Now, just enjoy the feelings of relaxation as they continue to deepen.

17. You also have the option at this stage of adding other exercises and/or vision statements (see below).

The more you practice this simple relaxation technique, the deeper you will go. The deeper you go the more you realize that this place of peace and power helps you enjoy your life more completely.

FREEMIND POWER PRACTICE 3

VISION STATEMENTS

A key part of reprogramming is using empowered language patterns. The following vision statements are very simple yet very powerful ways of creating space in your psychology so that you can enjoy more of your potential coming to life. Choose the statements that resonate with you, and repeat them while (ideally) being deeply relaxed (using the earlier relaxation exercises, see pages 167 and 169) or while going about your day in full waking consciousness. Repeating these vision statements to yourself last thing at night and first thing in the morning can really set you up for a beautiful day.

* Each and every day, I am feeling more and more confident.
* Each and every day, I believe in myself more and more.

* Each and every day, I accept myself more and more.
* Each and every day, I am enjoying feeling more and more fun and playful.
* With each day that passes, I am more and more capable of seeing the positive in all things.
* With each day that passes, I am noticing my listening skills are improving.
* The more I like myself the more I like my life; the more I like my life, the more I like myself.
* I am feeling more and more relaxed, each and every day.
* Each and every day, I am finding myself more and more motivated.
* Now I see all responses to me as opportunities for growth and learning.
* The more open I am, the more open I am to positive empowering change.
* Each and every day, I am becoming more and more aware of the benefits I offer to others.
* With every moment that passes, I am finding more and more ways to earn money.
* By day and by night, all my affairs are prospering.
* I am pleased with my natural ability and I trust myself more and more.
* Each and every day, my ability to enjoy every area of my life is improving.
* I am rich in spirit; I am rich in ability; I am wealthy.
* By day and by night, I am discovering new levels of happiness and contentment.
* Each and every day, I am improving in each and every way.
* Each and every day, I am being more and more compassionate/supportive/engaging/ inspiring (use any

word you want).

* Each and every conversation, I am speaking more and more effectively/dynamically/ assertively (use any word you want).
* With every moment that passes, I am more and more compassionate and open with myself and others.
* Each and every week, I am running my business/ department/work (use any word you want) more and more effectively and smoothly.
* Each and every night, I am sleeping more and more fully and getting more rest, leaving me more and more energized every day.
* Each and every day, I am treating my body with more and more respect.
* By day and by night, I love my body more and more.

FREEMIND POWER PRACTICE 4

MAGICAL ARM TWIST

It is fascinating to discover how much positive expectation (Success Psychology, see page 137) and visualization can enhance your performance. This small exercise is done without any kind of deep communication with your unconscious and yet the effect is incredible.

1. Stand up, making sure that you have plenty of space behind you, with your feet facing straight ahead. Then widen your stance a little and hold your **RIGHT** hand up, pointing your finger directly out in front of you.

2. Keeping your feet still, move your hand round to the
   RIGHT, twisting your body as you do, and continue this
   action until your hand has moved all the way around
   behind you. When you have got as far as you can, notice
   where you hand is pointing. Make a note of that position.

3. Untwist your body and come back to the center with
   your hands down by your sides. Now, look over your other
   shoulder, your **LEFT** shoulder, and look at that position
   you just pointed at.

4. Now, while still looking over your **LEFT** shoulder, imagine
   doing the exercise again and believe for a moment that
   this next time, because you are engaging the power of
   your mind, you will go further around. Pick a new 'target'
   that is a bit further round and take a moment to see
   yourself and feel yourself pointing at that new target.
   The more you can believe it, the more it will come true.
   You might want to close your eyes to imagine this fully.

5. Come back to center and twist your **RIGHT** arm round
   again to the **RIGHT** and see how far you get.

6. Now repeat steps 3 and 4 again, then try again and see if
   you can still go further.

This simple exercise gives you an inkling of the power of
focus, belief, and expectation.

FREEMIND POWER PRACTICE 5

MORNING RISE AND SHINE

As previously discussed, our expectations affect the
outcomes of what we do (see page 141), so it is a good idea to

visualize things going well *before* you do them. That doesn't mean that you should expect every situation to go your way. It is simply about expecting the best from yourself and being more relaxed in the world. The following exercise involves imagining what it is like to wake up in a great mood and have a great day. The visualization is best done last thing at night, but can be repeated all day long. For a deep experience, start at step 1 or for a quick boost simply start at step 4.

1. Relax your body as described in FreeMind Power Practices 1 and 2 (see pages 167 and 169) to come into the moment more and more.
2. Imagine yourself at the end of the following day having had a great day.[8]
3. Enjoy the feeling, and feel it in your body.
4. Think about how being your best self and looking after yourself and others is the best way to be happy.
5. Imagine yourself waking up in the morning feeling totally refreshed and raring to go.
6. Enjoy this feeling and amplify it until you can actually imagine the way it looks and feels.
7. See yourself, upon waking, throwing back the bed covers and happily springing out of bed.
8. See yourself at the end of the day, realizing that your good day is linked to your good mood in the morning.
9. Repeat the following vision statements (ideally feeling good feelings as you say them):
   * Each and every morning I am enjoying having more and more energy.
   * Each and every day I am experiencing more and more positivity.

* Each and every day I am enjoying helping myself feel
more and more alive.

10. If done last thing at night, allow yourself to drift off to
sleep very peacefully believing that the next day is
already taken care of. Trust the power of your mind and
relax into a deep and wonderful sleep. You are set for a
wonderful following day.

FREEMIND POWER PRACTICE 6

POSITIVE PERFORMANCES

There will always be times when you are put on the spot
– for example in exams, interviews, dates, and meetings –
especially if you are living fully and freely. So, this next
exercise is designed to help you ensure that, when it comes
to the crunch, you have the best chance possible of being
your best. By practicing being courageous, you guarantee
that, when good opportunities come your way, you will be
brave enough to take full advantage of them.

If you have enough time, use the complete exercise here
and steps 4 to 11 just before the event. However, any time
you want to boost your confidence quickly (sometimes we
get put on the spot with only minutes of warning) use steps
4 to 11 to help bring out the best from yourself.

1. Relax your body as described in FreeMind Power
Practices 1 and 2 (see pages 167 and 169) to come into
the moment more and more.

2. Put yourself in a positive frame of mind by thinking of a

time when you have done something well in the past.

3. See yourself just before beginning or entering this new challenge taking three magically relaxing deep breaths.

4. Let go of caring about the result – nothing is that important; relax any 'neediness' as best you can.

5. Take three deep breaths and relax more and more with each one.

6. See yourself at the end of the experience with it having gone well.[8]

7. Enjoy the experience, feeling proud and positive of who you are, and how you were true to yourself.

8. Feel and see yourself some time after the experience, still feeling pleased with how it went.

9. See yourself entering or beginning this situation looking calm and collected, breathing slowly and deeply.

10. Program your mind with the following vision statements, feeling positive emotions as you repeat them.

   * Each and every moment I am more relaxed about everything that happens.
   * Each and every day I am enjoying being myself more and more.
   * Each and every day I am feeling more and more confident and I am loving it.

11. In real life, before entering the experience, take three deep relaxing breaths and keep your mouth moist. This reduces adrenalin (nervousness and anxiety).

In life, we can't control how other people respond to us, but we can work on being the best version of ourselves. Then if we don't succeed, it doesn't matter because we can still put our heads on the pillow at night being pleased with who we are and what we are trying to achieve. This is the key to peace and happiness. It is also interesting that when you are in this place you are at your most relaxed, seem most confident, appear most attractive, and are perceived by others as being worthy of investment and trust.

Accepting yourself and being yourself is the secret to all success, but it can take practice to build up the courage to be yourself at all times. This exercise is full of techniques to help you do that more and more. After a while, you'll find that it becomes second nature to expect things to go well. This can really help you stay calm and deliver the best of yourself when it counts. This is the foundation of faith.

FREEMIND POWER PRACTICE 7

BRING YOUR VISION TO LIFE

This next exercise is a really effective technique for opening yourself up to new possibilities. If you want to change your life, you simply describe what a perfect day in your life would be like. You can also do this for the perfect partner or the perfect job. The idea is to describe, as vividly as possible, what it would be like to experience that life, that partner, or that job. The more description you add to your vision, the better.

You might choose to do this by creating a vision/dream board on your computer or a piece of card, using images from magazines that inspire you. It can also be really effective to write a description of who you would be in that world. Describe yourself and your ultimate potential as richly and as vividly as possible. Feel free to create a bright and colorful picture of this too. You might also want to add some inspiring vision statements to your images (see page 171). It can be very powerful to do this exercise before you use the other FreeMind reprogramming techniques.

When creating a vision for your life, if you want it to be really inspiring, you could add to your plan the positive impact you will have on others when you are living your dream. When we see our process of becoming our very best as an act of service, we wake up our heart and that is the most powerful part of ourselves for driving change. From there, we are not pushing ourselves simply for personal gain. Instead, as an act of service, we are leading ourselves to greatness.

*When we are motivated by love,
magical power moves through us.*

FREEMIND POWER PRACTICE 8

METAPHORICAL MUSICAL MAGIC

As discussed earlier, one of the most powerful ways to reprogram your mind is to use music as a metaphor (see page 160). Choose an inspirational piece of music and tell your inner mind (simply announce it) that this music is the sound of you bringing your best to life. You can be very specific. If you want to experience more confidence, more creativity, more relaxation, more productivity, or whatever it may be, you can simply decide that the next piece of music or the next album is the sound of that being increased. Then just put the music on and enjoy imagining the desired areas of your life being improved.

You can combine this with the other FreeMind Reprogramming visualization techniques. After using any of the other reprogramming techniques, it can be great to finish the experience by listening to a piece of powerful music. It works especially well if you move your body, visualize things going well, and repeat the vision statements (see page 171) at the same time.

Dancing is one of the quickest ways to embed new positive ideas and feelings. It can also be a really great way to start your day. You can, of course, use a specific piece of music to work on any particular issue that you might want resolved. That could be simply sending your body healing energy or getting direct insight around a relationship that is stuck. You simply tell yourself what you would like the music to mean and you will be astounded at what comes up. This technique sits at the core of all of the FreeMind recordings and it is incredibly powerful.

RECOMMENDED RESOURCES

MUSIC

* Craig Armstrong, *Balcony Scene*: A beautiful piece to visualize yourself coming out of difficulty and coming into the light.
* Dario Marianelli, *Elegy for Dunkirk*: Great for rousing your heart into action, this powerful motivational piece is full of pathos and passion. Use this to bring your heart's greatest vision to life.
* Ghostland, *Interview with an Angel*: A powerful motivational piece of music to use while you visualize things going well

for you. It can also be a great piece of music to finish off your reprogramming session.

BOOKS

* Deepak Chopra, *Ageless Body, Timeless Mind*
* Shakti Gawain, *Creative Visualization*
* Dr David Hamilton, *It's the Thought that Counts: Why Mind Over Matter Really Works*
* Joseph Murphy, *Power of the Subconscious Mind*

FREEMIND RESOURCES

* **FreeMind Power** A brief video on the power of the mind and how we can harness it to improve our lives. For more information, visit www.freemindproject.org/reprogramming or scan the QR code below.

* **FreeMind Home Training System** This helps to unleash your ultimate potential and harness the incredible power of your inner mind. Enjoy flowing with confidence, clarity, and charisma. The FreeMind training recordings combine all of the FreeMind Principles and Practices, with powerful hypnosis and metaphorically charged bespoke film score music. This home training system also includes short support and inspirational videos. For more information about the home training system see Further

FreeMind Resources, page 253, visit www.freemindproject.
org/3pillars, or scan the QR code below.

FreeMind Purpose: Reconnection

Peace and power (Pillars 1 and 2) are important but if they are not connected to a greater purpose, real and lasting happiness can still elude us. Therefore Pillar 3 is about connecting everything you do with a greater sense of purpose, and exploring the deeper aspects of what it really means to be part of a singular field of consciousness. Here we examine what I call 'Oneness Philosophy' to understand how our full and complete self-expression plays a part in the grand purpose of the evolution of the universe. As you begin to reconnect more to this perspective, unconditional love and happiness spreads through your whole life. We are filled with a light and a joy that is immediately obvious to everyone we come into contact with.

To be clear, Pillar 3 isn't about reconnecting to oneness. That connection can never be severed. It is simply about reconnecting your awareness of the interconnected nature of life. When we go from perceiving ourselves as a small, disconnected, limited, and fearful personality to understanding that we are the large, connected, unlimited, and joyful universality, everything begins to make sense. From there we can truly see the beauty and perfection in everything. This is the final YES of the Triple YES. This is the final pillar of absolute happiness.

ONENESS AT THE ATOMIC LEVEL

Our conscious minds have a limited capacity to perceive ourselves as being part of the singular field of consciousness. Fortunately science has now beautifully ratified what the ancient philosophers knew all those thousands of years ago. When I discovered that subatomic physics demonstrated that everything is interconnected, interdependent, and balanced, my epiphany felt completely supported and explained by science. The truth of all things, including us, is that everything is made up of atoms. Atoms are infinitesimally small. So small, in fact, that if you wanted to see the atoms that make up the parts of an orange, you would have to magnify that orange many times over. You would have to make it vast. In fact, if you made it the size of the Earth, each atom would still only be the size of a cherry in your hand.

Stop for a moment and consider how many cherries it would take to build a model of your house, or maybe a model of the town where you live? What about a model of the UK, Europe, or USA, or how many cherries it would take to fill the Pacific Ocean? Yes, inside every orange there are as many atoms as you would need numbers of cherries to build a model of the world. So, yes, atoms are very, very small, but even more amazing is that scientists have discovered that inside the atom there is a vast universe of space (about 99.99999999 percent of the atom's weight/mass is in the nucleus). The nucleus is a tiny, but heavy, speck in the middle of a vast expanse of comparative space.

To give you some idea of that scale, if an atom was magnified so that it was the size of the dome in London's St Paul's Cathedral (100ft across), then the nucleus would still only be the size of a grain of sand in the middle. This space, however, is not empty. It is filled with rapidly spinning electrons (light) circling around the center. Another way of seeing the scale would be to imagine a cat sat swinging a bee around itself on a piece of thread that was half a mile long. Yep, in every one of your cells, there are tens of millions of atoms, which are mainly spacious electromagnetic fields of light moving at 186,000 miles per second (at that speed light takes only eight minutes to travel 93 million miles from the sun to Earth). You are made purely of light. That is what everything is made of.

SPACE AND STUFF

To further illustrate the scale, imagine a bowl of puffed rice cereal (for example, Rice Krispies). The bowl would appear full but if you tipped the cereal out onto a surface and then flattened it with a rolling pin, the puffed grains of rice would soon be reduced to powder, which would fit easily into one teaspoon. And that is true of everything, but the scale is much more extreme. So, a world made of Rice Krispies may appear big but if all the space were squashed out of it the actual 'stuff' or hard 'matter' would compress to a much smaller size. The cereal analogy is useful for helping us understand the concept but the reality is much more exciting.

In the atomic arena, the ratio between space and stuff is so extreme that most people have trouble conceiving of the scale. I know I do. Science tells us that, if everything in the universe was squashed down and contracted back to its weighty atomic nucleus (had all the space removed), all the matter of the known universe would fit into the palm of a human hand! They reckon it would be the size of a pea. Yes, that's not just the Earth but also all the other planets and stars too! That should give you some idea of just how spacious we really are. We are vast expanses of mainly space, filled with extraordinarily rapidly spinning electromagnetic energy.

It is hard to imagine how heavy that pea would be. Just the weight of all the people in the UK or the USA standing on your hand is hard enough to comprehend. What about the weight of the Earth and the Sun — and that is just our solar system. The mind boggles to think of all that weight in something the size of a pea. Imagine how compact it would be — and very hot too. Apparently at the point of the Big Bang, when all of the matter was contracted, this heavy pea-sized ball would have been 18 billion, million, million, million degrees Fahrenheit. That is also very hard to comprehend. However, the following helps put this into perspective.

Imagine placing a soccer-ball-sized sphere of stone into a fire and leaving it there until it went red-hot, all the way through to its center. If you removed it from the fire, it would take a long time to cool down. After a while the surface of the stone would be cool but the middle would still be incredibly hot. Well, this describes the Earth perfectly. This stone sphere has been out of that fire for over 13.7 billion years and yet it still hasn't fully cooled down. The surface is cool enough to live on, but at the core it is still molten. What an extraordinary heat it must have been to begin with for it still, after all these years, to be that hot on the inside.

What gets really fascinating about the atomic world is how space and light behave. Traditional science, which sees things as distinct and separate, cannot reconcile the true nature of what happens in the atom. Inside the atom, all the particles behave as if they are all permanently connected. Even when they are seemingly separate and acting independently, they respond in correlation with each other and simultaneously. So, it isn't like communication travels from one side of the atom to the other to effect change. The changes happen instantaneously. These findings completely challenge traditional scientific models of understanding the world but support the principle of interconnected oneness that the ancients have been talking about for millennia. In other words, you, me, this book, that tree, and that office building over there are all part of the same stuff and intrinsically connected as parts of a greater whole.

....

QUANTUM ENTANGLEMENT

There is one fascinating experiment,[9] in particular, which has drawn huge global attention to these phenomena. Scientists managed to split a particle of light (a photon) into two particles. They then shot both 'twin' particles in opposite directions down 7 miles of fiber-optic cabling. At the end of the cable, there were a series of junctions where the particles had the choice to go left or right. These particles were now separated (according to the standard mechanical understanding of the world) by over 14 miles, but at each junction, every time, they both acted in complete correlation. They made their way through the duplicate junction maze in exactly the same way, at exactly the same time, every single time.

The scientists call this quantum entanglement, and it has rocked the foundations of mechanical science. On the atomic level, once something has been joined it remains connected and continues to interact interdependently, even though to our senses it appears separate. Bear in mind that everything that makes us up and everything in the known universe was once one very small sphere of intensely connected matter. There was a time when we truly were one with everything. Just like the photon this split. Now things seem separate, but we are still connected. Science doesn't know how yet, but they have proven this to be so. They have now tested these synchronized connections over much longer distances and the truth of universal interconnection is being borne out.

....

So to recap

1. Light is in everything; it is the substance of all matter.
2. Light is the power that drives everything.
3. Light is permanently connected. In other words, it knows what every other part of itself is doing and responds accordingly, immediately.

By that description light (everything/God) is omnipresent, omnipotent, and omniscient. This scientific knowledge totally ratified my firsthand experience of the interconnected oneness, which I described in Part I (see Chapter 1, page 3).

Does that mean you are not in this universe but instead actually a part of this universe? Yes!

Does this mean that you are part of a singular field of reality that cannot be threatened, wrong, out of place, inadequate, lost or broken? Yes!

Does that mean that whatever you have ever thought that is contrary to that idea is an imaginary inadequacy that may be unnecessarily causing you trouble? Yes!

Does that mean that by some description you are God? Yes!

Does that mean that you shouldn't get too excited because so is your carpet? Yes!

Could it be that if you aligned yourself with the experience of the universe and yourself as part of that perfection then you would relax and have a much better time of it? Yes!

Is it possible that you could do that now? Yes.

Is it easy? No.

THE SPIRITUAL JOURNEY

It was amazing to discover that, without the science to back them up, the ancients had come to understand these supernatural truths. And so I began to look at spiritual texts differently. I began seeing them as attempts to convey these wonderful and simple enlightening truths. I started seeing through the metaphors and understanding the beauty in the wisdom they were trying to promote. One day I asked myself the question, 'Well, if God or the universe is really just another word for "light," how might the Bible read if, wherever it said "God" or talked about the world, I replaced it with the word "light" instead?'

To answer the question, I picked up a Bible and the opening sentence of Genesis made me laugh aloud. I didn't need to replace anything. The Bible is packed full of references to the light and being at one with it: 'Let there be light,' 'be a light unto yourself,' 'turn to the light,' 'I am the light of the lord,' 'at-one-ment,' to mention just a few. This was an absolute revelation to me. All my life I had dismissed religion as nonsense and here I was realizing that it was my confusion around the concept of God that was causing the problem.

I remember when I first dismissed religion as nonsense. I was seven and attending West House School in Birmingham in the UK. There was an act of worship and we were being told about the devil tempting Jesus in the desert. I just didn't buy it. Something about a separate demon didn't feel right, so I dismissed the whole thing as nonsense. However, my experience might have been quite different if someone had explained that spirituality is about our journey to come to terms with our natural selfish desires; or had explained that the story (like all great stories) was a way of helping me to realize that true happiness lies in giving rather than taking. Had it been explained to me that we have fear inside ourselves, which can twist us into competitive and controlling demons that bring only darkness to the world, well then maybe, just maybe, I would have understood that religion had something to offer me.

That is the spiritual journey and it is the source of the greatest happiness we can find. That is the home of all true freedom, but that journey itself (like all good stories) is fraught with great difficulty and danger. This is the hero's journey that we are all on.

The meaning of life is to go from selfish to selfless. To operate from love, not fear.

SETTING OUT ON THE JOURNEY

Many people live and die without ever discovering the joy and happiness that comes from consciously taking this journey. In all of the major religions of the world, ancient esoteric texts all speak about oneness and enlightenment. In Judaism, there is the Kabbalah, in Islam there is Sufism, in Christianity there is the Gospel according to Thomas, and the non-dual text called the Cloud of Unknowing. In Hinduism there is Advaita and the extraordinarily precise teachings of Kashmir Shaivism. In Chinese philosophy, there is Taoism. In Buddhism, the philosophy centers around theories and practices about oneness and enlightenment. Generally as religions became more organized, they became more dogmatic and some of these core simple truths got lost along the way. However, when you study some of the older, more esoteric texts the similarities between all of these approaches is stupefying. The single message really is deafening.

How the spiritual journey is described varies wildly and ideas about the best way to walk that path also vary massively, but underneath the cultural differences the journey of the human heart and its liberation from fear is the same the world over. Water is the same the world over too, but internationally goes by many different names. How it is fetched, carried, and treated varies hugely too. Some people have to traipse five miles a day and back just to fill their buckets with enough water to survive, while others have water pumped directly into their homes. Some people's natural water supply has dried up, and other people's water has become infected or poisonous and has the capacity to do them great harm. In some places, the water has had extra things added to it to make it 'better for you,' according to what certain people think you need. In some places, the water has been recycled and regurgitated and treated so many times that it is full of things that were never there to begin with. Some creatures have lived in water their whole lives and therefore never question it, while others are so immersed in it they don't even know it exists.

Spirituality and the path of becoming self-aware go by many different names too. How religion and God are described worldwide also varies vastly. It goes by many different names and is fetched, carried, valued, and understood differently all over the world. Some people see it, some people don't, some people were born into it, so they don't question it, and in some places people add things to spirituality to make it different and 'better for you,' according to their idea of what is good for you. Many of us have also seen people be so poisoned by it that we wouldn't want to go anywhere near it. It is worth being careful where we get our water but it is equally important to respect and understand that while people might be using different names for their spiritual journey, while they may have different practices or seemingly different values, we are all on the same path and every path is deserving of love and respect.

ABSOLUTE PERFECTION

All things, including ourselves, are material expressions of a singular field that is a matrix of interdependent forces that act according to physical laws – which means the universe operates in a balanced and perfect way. The balance cannot be broken. The perfection remains untarnished and yet in its expressed material form it is evolving all the time. That balance can be expressed in harmony or dysfunction, growth and entropy, creation and dissolution, simplicity and complexity. There is not some master plan or blueprint but there is a set of physical laws that determine how that balance is maintained. There is no outside agency running the show, no external mind able to reach in and intervene. There is no points system by which we can earn our right to be looked after. There is simply the ever-present capacity within all of us to relax into the flow of this evolution and find joy in being part of the process. This happens most clearly when we have the courage to live in truth and love.

For hundreds of reasons, many of which are based on simple social and philosophical logic, it is clear that being lovely and truthful is the quickest way to bless yourself and your life. You don't need to believe in a perfectly balanced and interconnected interdependent matrix of light energy to understand that being peaceful, honest, and loving makes your life immeasurably more wonderful. The evidence for that is everywhere and the more we can believe that, the better.

The degree to which we believe we are blessed is the degree to which we are blessed.

All the spiritual texts reference a saint or enlightened person being safe from harm. Be it called 'grace,' 'blessedness,' or 'what have you,' this concept turns up in a number of places. The idea that you could walk through the jungle and the wildest beasts would not attack you is a very common theme:

Those who are filled with life need not fear tigers and rhinos in the wilds,
Nor wear armor and shields in battle;
The rhinoceros finds no place in them for its horn,
The tiger no place for its claw,
The soldier no place for a weapon,
For death finds no place in them.

Lao-Tzu, Tao Te Ching

THE SPIRITUAL PARADOX

People often talk about dogs being able to smell fear (adrenalin), making them more likely to attack. In the wild, the runt of the litter is often devoured by its own siblings. It is a very harsh way of keeping the pack and the bloodline strong. We can see the same game play out in our human interactions. We don't eat insecure people but they certainly don't flourish in the same way. Perhaps, this is the singular field searching for ever-more perfect material expressions of itself. This is evolution of the field of consciousness. From that perspective the rules are simple. Peace represents good design and fear represents poor design. Those people who are most at peace are those who are best adapted to their environment. Those who are living in fear are the ones who are struggling. The most advanced form of peace is enlightenment and that state of mind can only be experienced and maintained when it is based on an awareness of the interconnected truth of reality.

When we truly experience oneness we see no separation or difference in anything. All is one. If we had that perspective and found ourselves blissfully floating through a jungle and came across a lion, we would be perfectly relaxed about being eaten. From a truly 'oneness' perspective that person may, while being eaten, be pleased that they (as the lion) were having a good lunch. They would identify as much with the lion as they do with themselves. The lion and the lunch would be one and the same.

To change forms and have atoms in one part of the condensed oneness be disassembled in human form and then reassembled in lion form wouldn't make much difference to the enlightened being (or the atoms either). We are collections of atoms of the food we have eaten. Here, however, is the interesting point. If we could really be at that much peace then when a lion happened upon us it probably wouldn't see us as food. That is the kicker – the beautiful spiritual paradox.

When we no longer require anything, we receive all the blessings. When we no longer care about being eaten, we aren't attacked. When we are ultimately at peace, in need of nothing, then everything is delivered. The reverse is also borne out. When we need things, and desperately push and shove in despair, nothing seems to work. We are unattractive, more likely to be mugged, less likely to be loved, more likely to be overlooked for promotion, less likely to get a partner, less likely to succeed, prosper, and travel widely. Our seed, which is much less likely to be welcome, if placed at all, will not fall far from the tree. The world's wisdom traditions and the FreeMind Experience are summarized in the following principle.

Be at peace and thrive.
Be in fear and struggle.

To me, at least, these seem to be the rules of the game. You could sit in any café in the world, paying attention to people's interactions and see this phenomenon at play every day. Think about those moments when things have gone well for you, and it's likely that you will find that you can track your greatness back to your peace. Times perhaps when you were more loving, truthful, and relaxed. In the same way, we can track our disasters back to our fears that fed our need to control, our attachment to outcomes, our need for a specific result, or our general resistance to 'what is and what might be.' That tension is tangible and it attracts the very worst to us.

What does your world look like right now? How are your relationships? Are you at peace with yourself? How are things working? Are people attacking you? Humans tend to attack those things we dislike most in ourselves. The weak are the most vicious in their (often mob) attack on other people's failings. The tabloid press is an expression of that collective desire to persecute weakness. To relish in the fall of the 'great' is to crucify the weakness that we fear most in ourselves.

And what of the reverse, the true acceptance of ourselves, the total acceptance of the moment, the complete and utter alignment with 'what is,' including our own inevitable dissolution? To walk as if the lion has already eaten you is to be in connection with eternal life. Atoms change form but every part of us is as old as the Earth. We are all 13.7 billion years old. When your identity is aligned with your singular universality, the associated awareness of the ever-present can bring total and complete peace with 'what is.' That is the ultimate FreeMind Experience and in that place we are all blessed.

When we are afraid the body releases adrenalin into our system and causes the fight-or-flight response. We are programmed at our most basic physical level to push away, challenge, or even, at times, attack people when they are releasing adrenalin. Our conscious and unconscious minds would like things to be cozy and easy for us. That's very understandable but it is that part of the mind that balks at life when it is difficult. So, it can be very useful to get comfortable with the idea that life is meant to be challenging. Dropping the hope for things to be easy makes it easier to start enjoying the process of being challenged. You might even work on making yourself resilient so that you can remain relaxed and positive while things are difficult. I encourage all my clients to see life as a character gym: A place where we lift the weights of difficulty and develop our emotional, psychological, and spiritual fitness.

For example, you could see life as a stress test where the universe is looking for good design. If you are thriving in life you could be considered to be a good design that has adapted well. If, in contrast, you start to feel fearful and resist things then you will be releasing adrenalin, which gives the signal for others to push you away or attack you. Adrenalin is evidence of bad design or bad adaptation. The resultant attack is the way in which the universe is destroying and disassembling the poorly designed or poorly adapted mechanism. This is no longer about you fighting off predators and running fast. This is not about necessarily being so strong and invincible that you can overpower your oppressors or fight off the lions. It is about peacefully and lovingly relaxing into the truth of your real nature.

From the perspective of fear, life is cruel and hard. From the perspective of love, life is an opportunity to develop the capacity to enjoy peace and freedom. It is true, therefore, that the meek may still inherit the Earth but only if they can just be at peace with not inheriting the Earth (and possibly being eaten too).

It can be useful to see the universe as a stress test in search of good design, but I prefer to see it more simply as an opportunity for reconnection. In all the spiritual texts the theme of return, reconnection, or reabsorption appears often. Some think that the joy of love and the bliss of connection can only be experienced in contrast to disconnection and conflict. The divine only knows itself as the divine by losing itself, and finding itself over and over again. Some say this is why God created man, so that he could forget himself and rediscover himself time and time again. Our struggles then are the hurdles that make us jump higher. They are simply opportunities for transcendence and remembrance.

THE END OF MORALITY AND NON-DUALITY

There is nothing separate from you; there is not one thing that is indistinguishable from anything else. This singular field is our entirety and between every single breath, if we choose, we can feel our interconnectedness with everything. This truth vibrates through every one of our cells in every single moment of life's re-expression of itself. Our perceived boundaries are nothing more than blurred perceptions that see variations in density as separate and distinct objects. We are the perceptual mechanisms – the feedback loops of the singular field of consciousness that is exploring ever more elegant forms of expression. In that place, you are not your name nor your age or your gender. Beyond the familiar sense of 'you' there is a much bigger sense of 'YOU' that is everything that has ever been. In that place you are the intelligence that makes the sun rise and the oceans swell. You are the alpha and the omega.

One is all we are. One is all we have ever been. One is all we will ever be.

Whether we are aware of it or not, we ache for a pure moment of expression when we lose ourselves in the moment, flowing without conscious awareness and something beautiful (artful/ divine) flows through us. A clear and perfect utterance or reflection of a vibration that resonates so powerfully with who we are, and what the moment calls for, that we both disappear and arrive at exactly the same time. That small sense of separate self dissolves away to leave us feeling more present than ever. That force and flow of purity seeking its own reflection in our actions has been aching through us for the last 13.7 billion years.

Close your eyes for one moment and you will feel the millennia twitching throughout your whole system – our ancient atoms are alive with pure unbridled light energy that craves reabsorption into the greater whole. The experience of one cosmic constant resonating vibration of home, of freedom, of being found, connected, whole, and complete. This is our journey, our only purpose, and all our other attempts to make meaning or find peace in this world will fall short if they are not informed and driven by this simple and beautiful awareness of our eternal oneness.

In a world operating without much practical awareness of the interconnected nature of reality, you may be able to feel that something is misaligned in the core of your being. It may feel as though there is a core corruption in the very structure of what is being peddled to you as the 'normal way of things' – a dark oddity of illogical nonsense that everyone seems to be going along with. A stirring nausea that begs you to stop, pleads with you to pause for a moment to feel the true power of your being, the real purpose of life and the joy, awe and wonderment of your true self. There is a deep calling to step outside of those culturally imposed imaginings, those toxic crushing normalities and formalities, which can stew the human soul in the most dark and sorry flavor. But for all of that social conditioning, the crooked values, and false posturing, our connection is not lost, we are not something separate that can be cut away. It is only our perception of that connection that can be lost. I can say without any reservation that the meaning of life is the rediscovery and re-experience of the interconnected nature of reality – that is the home of all peace and all power. That ultimately is our purpose.

It is very possible that you have become numb to the natural part of you that would protest at the so-called normal world. You may have ignored your calling for an expression of something more beautiful for so long that you can no longer hear the invitation. You may have simply become incredibly philosophical or spiritual about accepting the world is as it is. That may also have slipped into a total apathy underpinned by a sorry sense of impotence. You may be wholly aware that having more rich and varied sensory experiences doesn't really compensate for the loss of something more important. You may be painfully aware that buying more things doesn't make a jot of difference to that feeling of hollowness inside. So many of us know that there is something deeper being called forward from within us. There is something pure, beautiful, and perfect waiting to be expressed, reflected, and realized. There is some crystalline purpose longing to be fulfilled. Your perfect greatness is very ready to be delighted in its 'Self.'

RECONNECTING TO ONENESS

The FreeMind Purpose Practices (see page 223) are designed to enable you to reconnect to that sense of oneness. As you allow that perspective of perfection to slowly filter through your life, you can't help but start to see your own inherent perfection. That is what will enable you to start enjoying more authenticity and self-expression. That is what will enable you to start living and loving fully. In that place, you will be more present, passionate, and playful. In your own enthusiasm (filled with divine energy) for yourself and life, you will naturally become an expression of divine beauty and your life will be filled with great happiness, abundance, and joy.

This return to, or this re-expression of, your most divine nature is not something you can choose to do or not. You can simply become aware of the process that is happening anyway. Every experience of your life is a reflection of that process. It is happening whether you like it or not. The quality of your life, the nature of how you feel, the positivity of your relationships, the satisfaction you feel at work, the degree to which what you think, say, and do are aligned, the degree to which people trust you, and the degree to which you trust yourself are all reflections of your awareness of your true nature. If you currently feel that your life is lacking in meaning then I invite you to realize that there is meaning in everything. If a person is disheartened it is usually because they are leading a life that they feel is hollow and empty; the very dissatisfaction they are feeling is the source of the meaning. The suffering is the invitation. The perfect game still plays out.

Sadness occurs because of the distance between the reality of our life and the potential life our heart knows we could be enjoying.

However, let's be really clear. This is not about 'good' and 'bad,' 'right' and 'wrong.' There is not one life, one career, one job, or one relationship that is necessarily better than any other. There is no judgment or overarching morality that values one thing over another. You may enjoy one way of living more than another way but I invite you to experience that simply as a preference. The world of morality is the miserable and judgmental, gossipy, malicious, and competitive world of 'should,' 'shouldn't,' 'must,' 'mustn't,' 'ought to,' 'oughtn't to,' 'need to' and 'needn't.' These judgmental structures of duality underpin our sense of separation, and I believe it to be the source of all fear and suffering. Letting go of the idea that one thing is better than another is an essential part of finding true freedom.

According to the principles of Oneness Philosophy, there is no distinguishing one thing over another. Everything is part of the singular field, so nothing has more value than anything else. This is called the 'dissolving of duality' and it is really good news because that means nothing actually matters. There is no real right and wrong. There is no longer a scale of morality upon which to judge ourselves or others. There simply is 'what is.' We make up the meaning about whether what is happening is OK or not. That is our doing, our imagining. Yes, we can suffer by the meaning we choose but essentially, with practice, we can move beyond seeing things as good or bad. We can see beyond the seeming variety. We can stop viewing reality from the perspective of the suffering mind, which continually compares things. The conscious mind is either moving away from 'bad' stuff (aversion) or moving toward 'good' stuff (attraction). Everything is judged and either loved or resisted. Welcomed or pushed away. Everything welcomed is susceptible to the fear of being lost. And everything resisted is susceptible to the fear of returning.

The conscious mind goes round and round buying into 'one thing being one thing' and 'another thing being another.' When we see all things as equal, things that are outside of us no longer determine our mood. When we understand things from a wider, universal perspective the concepts of good and bad become totally redundant. This principle is demonstrated in the following story.

....

A FARMER'S LUCK

One day a farmer felt compassion for his old and tired horse so he let his horse run free. The other villagers said, 'What a shame. Now your only horse is gone. How unfortunate you are! How will you work and survive?'

The farmer replied, 'Who knows? We shall see.'

Two days later the old horse came back and was followed by two young healthy wild horses. Now the villagers said, 'How fortunate you are! You must be very happy!'

Again, the farmer replied softly, 'Who knows? We shall see.'

The next morning, the farmer's only son began training the new wild horses, but he was thrown to the ground and broke his leg. Now the villagers said, 'Oh, what a tragedy! Your son won't be able to help you farm. How will you survive? You must be very sad.'

The farmer calmly went about his business and answered, 'Who knows? We shall see.'

Several days later a war broke out and the Emperor's men arrived in the village demanding that the young men be conscripted into the Emperor's army. As it happened the farmer's son was deemed unfit because of his broken leg and was saved from a war that killed many of the other young men from the village.

....

THE EGO IDENTITY AND ITS ATTACHMENT TO SUFFERING

Fear and the attendant resistance make us grasp for control. We hatch a plan, create a strategy, hope for the best, and imagine that we know what 'best' is. This also includes choosing a way of being that we think will help us manage, cope, or adapt to life. Over time this becomes an identity that we can become overly attached to, but that identity may prevent us from being fully present in the moment. Our conditioning or our idea of ourselves can block our ability to be truly free in the moment. This ego identity or fearful personality has very rigid ideas about what is good and bad. This attachment to things being a certain way is a huge source of suffering.

The fearful personality is addicted to thinking that everything will be OK when they have x, y, and z; and when a, b, and c does or doesn't happen – essentially when something external is different. Maybe if we have more of one thing and less of another, then we will be OK? Maybe it is the ideal partner, or that happiness will come with a dishwasher, or when our partner acts more like a dishwasher. Whatever we think will bring us happiness usually only ever fuels the furnace of dissatisfaction that is all too ready to burn painfully inside us.

Happiness and contentment can only come about when we no longer identify with that part of our consciousness that thinks we are separate. In that world of duality and judgment, suffering is unavoidable because all that thinking holds in place the primary feeling of things not being good enough. If things need to be different, so do we. This underpins all of the shunning, grasping, judging, condemning, competitive, and critical thoughts, feeling and behaviors that only go to further deepen our feelings of inadequacy and isolation. This is the vicious circle of egoist misery that is the driving force behind the record-breaking amount of antidepressants that so many people consume these days.

The end of morality doesn't lead to an outcropping of anarchic, dangerous, and destructive behavior. Far from it. The end of morality frees people from the condemnation of self and other, so that they can finally relax into who they actually are. Not because they 'should' but because they 'can.' When people stop pushing themselves to be good with 'shoulds' and 'musts,' they begin to relax and discover that at their core they are naturally inclined to live in harmony with themselves and others. This breeds more peace and love and that only goes to make all of our lives much easier and considerably more enjoyable.

FREE WILL

When we identify more with the singular field of consciousness, then the world of morality becomes more and more redundant because we begin to see that we are not really in control of our choices or our actions. Yes, we can choose how we respond to what we think, feel, and do, but we don't really have much choice about what we think, feel, and do. The limited personality (ego) really likes to believe that it has free will and gets very upset at the idea that it is not in control. We must surely all be in control, otherwise what is the point of making effort, or trying to be good, or getting out of the bed in the morning? That is the point. There is no point. Not in the absolute sense. Everything is equal. One thing is not more meaningful than anything else. It doesn't matter. That doesn't render things meaningless. In fact that principle gives us freedom.

So, what would you like to do? What do you feel drawn to do in this moment? But don't worry because you are not really about to decide. Not in a free will, open choice kind of a way. The thoughts and feelings you have and the behaviors you choose are outside of your control. Everything you are thinking about, as you are engaging with this idea, is not chosen by you – the thoughts, retorts, resistances, or agreements are surfacing in your awareness and you are simply noticing them. You are not planning to think your next thought. It just turns up. You are not planning your next mood or emotion. They just turn up.

If you disagree and want to believe that you do have control over which thoughts and feelings arise in your mind, those thoughts and feelings are still a product of the conditioning that you received. The parenting you received affected your model of the world. Your DNA determines your level of intelligence and your ability to apply that intelligence is a reflection of the education you received. The culture of the country and the community you were brought up in has a huge impact on your needs and desires. You had no control over any of these factors. The choices we make, the thoughts we think, the feelings we feel, and the ways we behave are all a product of things we had no control over. That means by definition that our choices are not truly our own.

The pioneering neuroscience research done by Benjamin Libet has now proven[10] that when we decide consciously to do something, our unconscious had already decided beforehand. The parts of the brain that start the action happening – such as getting up to use the bathroom or put the kettle on – begin a whole second or so before you consciously think, 'Oh, I need the bathroom' or 'I want a cup of tea.' In our conscious mind, we think we have just had that thought. In truth, we are just witnessing something that has already been decided upon and is in the process of being actioned already.

We are not in control. What a relief. That simple fact, if considered fully, can lead to the total forgiveness of everyone for anything and everything they have ever done to you. The conscious mind will still constantly strategize and assess. It will always be caught up with attraction and aversion, and will always relate to itself as though it is really in control and there is some 'right' and 'wrong' way to go. Appreciate that part of your consciousness because it is doing what it feels it needs to do to get by. It is, however, very little to do with who you actually are. It is a life-management mechanism that has become so familiar with its own sense of self that it has many people convinced that they ARE that personal choice-making mechanism.

Believe it or not, this is not a denial of your power to make decisions. It is simply an invitation for you to recognize that your true power, or agency, comes from your universal mind. That is actually who you are. That is the 'You' that is also 'Me.' The 'You' that is everything. That intelligence is infinitely creative, responsive, ever evolving, and ultimately powerful. The small 'you' – which is defined by your name, age, gender, social conditioning, personal fears, and various compensatory strategies for survival – is not truly able to choose or control anything. At best it is a witness.

You can, of course, decide to be a happy witness trusting all is well (faith); or you can imagine there is a problem that you need to fix (fear), and suffer imagining that what is and isn't happening is a reflection of your failings. This is the source of misplaced guilt at times of difficulty, and misplaced pride at times of success. Our small personal self isn't responsible for our failings or our successes. Many people resist this idea but, in fact, our greatest joy is to be found in realizing our truly powerful universal nature. That is blissful freedom.

....

GRIEF LOVES LIFE:
DEATH CONNECTS US DEEPLY TO YES

I was totally devastated when I first heard my maternal grandmother had died. She was so passionate about making the most of life. She awoke a passion in me for amazing movies and delicious seafood. I wept at her funeral and felt a deep love for her, but then very soon felt at peace with her death. However, it was only a few years later when the grief struck me again that I came to understand death in a deeper way.

I was at the movie theater and I saw the wonderful *Something's Gotta Give* with Jack Nicholson and Diane Keaton. She would have absolutely loved it. I thought about her as the credits rolled and suddenly out of nowhere I dropped into a vast sea of grief. I wept as I realized she was never going to see that movie. This idea hurt so much. There was nothing that could be done about that. She was never going to see so many things. She never got to meet my daughter, her great-granddaughter. She was going to miss so many other great movies, so many great stories, and so many delicious lobsters. It soon became clear that I wasn't crying for her. I was crying for myself.

· ·

Do you ever stop to think of all the amazing things you will never see? All the amazing movies you won't enjoy or the incredible music you won't ever hear. What about the family members that you won't meet and get to love? The weddings you won't be part of. The foods you won't taste. The years of life you won't have. The central heart of grief is a deep love of life. This led me to realize that funerals should be the most important rituals in our lives. The best honoring for the dead is for their death to be a reminder of what is wonderful about life. A great funeral should make us all remember that life is short. That life is precious. We should be sat in a funeral and asking ourselves, 'Why the hell am I working at this job that I hate?' 'Why am I staying in this relationship that is not fulfilling me?' Life is so short. This is not bad or sad news. If we are breathing, we could be celebrating every breath.

If you were unfortunate enough to have your head submerged under water against your will, I'd imagine that you would try to live. Your hands grabbing at the hand pushing you down, trying to break yourself free; the feeling of panic that would increase as you struggled for breath, an imprisoned gasp fighting for life. Anger and energy would erupt and a true frenzied fight would explode. Finally you would fight yourself free and break the surface of the water, and that first breath of air would be incredibly valuable to you.

We are all about 60 seconds away from realizing how much we love life. Why do we have to be submerged under water for a minute for our true love of life to become clear? That desperation for air is a very real thirst for life. Do you bring that enthusiasm to your daily life? Is your life a reflection of your true love of life? In the past I have been asked to do some work with people who are dying. So far, I have never been asked to go to the deathbed of anyone who could say they had lived fully. Helping someone reconcile with the fact that they haven't made the most of their life is very difficult. In that situation, the only thing that makes sense is to encourage them to use the remainder of their time to convince their loved ones to grab life with both hands and make the necessary changes required to enjoy their life to the full. Plan to be at peace on your deathbed by making the most of this precious life now. To explore this further, try the 'deathbed questionnaire' (see page 229).

The only difference between a rut and a grave is depth.
Aboriginal proverb

EVERLASTING LIFE

The idea of eternal life has been promoted by many of the world's religions but it is usually described as being a heaven that we go to which is somewhere else. However, the eternal life described by those original seers was, as far as I can see, not about somewhere that you go to after this life. It was not about an afterlife. I believe they were trying to convey the truth of our ever-present life, which is eternal. After all, science has shown that we are all part of a singular field of light energy, which is about 13.7 billion years old. We know we are made up of a vast co-mingling of atoms. Therefore connecting to our eternal and universal essence is a matter of getting beyond our ego's perception of itself as an identity, a separate thing that can therefore live and die.

The ever so slightly more condensed corner of this ocean of mass, which I imagine to be me, is just an idea that has developed through the nature of this temporary contraction into form. In truth, we are not born, we are simply re-formed in all sorts of seemingly variable forms. There is no birth and therefore no death. We are one soup playing at making different shapes. Take a large pool of pure water and throw in seven billion ice cubes shaped like humans and made of the exact same water. Throw in many billions of animal-shaped ice cubes and many trillions of insect-shaped ice cubes. Imagine all those supposedly different 'beings' imagining themselves distinct and separate from everyone else. We are one wonderfully varied soup of light energy playing itself into many seemingly different forms.

When we can identify with the interconnected field all of our fears dissolve away. This is the core of spiritual transformation. Our ego structure relaxes and goes from being alone and lost, to being connected and loved. This deep sense of connection is felt, life feels eternal and a very powerful YES erupts out of this place and we learn that through surrender we get everything we ever wanted. That is the light at the end of the tunnel. Once here, you can dissolve your deepest resistance to death, so that you can finally allow life in all its glory to happen. The word religion derives from the Latin word 're-legere,' which means 'reconnect.' In the Indian traditions the word that sums up religious process is 'yoga' and that literally means 'to join.' Reconnection is the final pillar of the FreeMind Experience and it is a vital part of living and loving life to the full. (See page 226 for a visualization exercise that you can use to work on this yourself.)

Once we are connected all the fears that drive our negative behavior fall away. From there we naturally become heavenly. That is our paradise and that is available right now and forevermore.

When we get connected, we simply want to be more loving to ourselves and others. Your heart wants to reach out in love, to step up, to step into that potential that you know is calling you forth. To set things right, to let things go, to give everyone around you permission to be exactly who they are. There is enough love and food to go around. In this place we allow our shoulders and eyebrows to relax. We breathe deep into our bellies and bring a big universal YES to the world. We are finally OK with how it is now, and are finally in love with everything that has brought us to where we are. We become a channel of unconditional love by simply being an example of someone in love with themselves and their life. That is both our opportunity and our responsibility. This and this alone is our true purpose.

ACTIVISM IN THE FIELD
OF PERFECTION

So many people feel it is their social responsibility to 'do' something to make the world a better place. Perhaps you want to dig wells in Africa, or give money to a children's charity, or computers to the Third World. All of that is wonderful, of course, but how might the world be improved if we all just worked on ourselves? Letting go of our personal pain, letting go of our resentments, letting our heart become as big as it wants to without fear of how we may look, or how people may take advantage. How might we raise our children then? How might we run businesses? How might we inspire each other? How might our world work more beautifully? I suspect that the wells in Africa that need to be dug will then be dug, the right computers will go to the right places, and the right charities will be generously supported.

Love, care, and attention will spring better on the wings of our personal enthusiasm than they will under the strife and struggle of our dour responsibility.

BUT SHOULDN'T WE DO
SOMETHING ABOUT THE WORLD?

As I described earlier in the book (see page 69), there was a time in my journey when I began to believe that it was my job to save the world. I forgot the 'perfection,' and began to see the world as having serious problems. I respect my original intention hugely but on this new path I discovered the wisdom behind the proverb, 'The road to hell is paved with good intentions.' I was no longer at peace, bringing love and happiness to the world. I had a furrowed brow and was fighting the system. It was only when everything came crumbling down that I realized that it was my perspective that was the problem.

One of my dearest friends, Brian, used to say, 'There is nothing wrong with the world. We are just having a strange conversation.' I struggled with this concept for a long time. I felt I could see real problems in the world. After a while, I realized something about human development, which now helps me feel much more relaxed when I look at the world. For example, most teenagers go through a stage of being *erm* ... idiots. They can be rude, churlish, rebellious, disrespectful, and wholly unpleasant. This is not true of all teens, but is certainly true of many. This, however, is not evidence that something is out of place and broken. It is evidence that they are teenagers. It is in fact simply a very healthy stage in a child's development.

I now feel exactly the same way about human consciousness. Yes, terrible things are happening and as a race we could be so much more wise and mature, but right now I reckon we are basically very young. Like a teenager (or possibly even a bit younger) trying to find its way. I am not placing myself above or beyond that age either. In the general vibration of my consciousness, I can totally feel that on some days I am moments away from a big teenage tantrum. Is humanity therefore bad? Do we need to fight to make it different? Or is it instead possible that we are in a healthy (but unpleasant, for others at least) stage of development? Are we not just finding our way exactly as would be expected of a young child?

I don't think that feeling bad, wrong, or guilty will help. In fact I am certain that will hold in place many of the loathed characteristics that we would otherwise move beyond naturally. Recycle if it makes you feel good. Be a better boss if that's what inspires you. Campaign for change if you come alive in the process, but don't fight and fret to make a difference. That will only make things worse.

> *Don't ask yourself what the world needs, ask yourself what makes you come alive, and then go do that. Because what the world needs is people who have come alive.*
> Harold Thurman Whitman

LOVE AT CONTINUOUS SIGHT

If you had two rings and they both weighed exactly the same, and both were made of 24-carat gold, a jeweler would value them at exactly the same price. It wouldn't matter if one ring was beautiful and the other one was ugly. Once melted down, the substance they are made from is exactly the same. If, as you go about living your life, you remember this simple analogy it may help you see the inherent perfection in all things. It is easy to see the perfection in a child's smile but not so easy to see that same perfection in the mangled wreck of a car crash. What if both were made of 24-carat gold? The more I worked with the idea that we can't possibly know what is supposed to happen, the more I realized that the enlightened position is one of trusting that all things are golden, even if at first glance they don't appear to be. On the days when I experience that perspective it is like being in love. Everything is accorded the same appreciation. Everything you see, you look upon with love. It is love at continuous sight.

Some people may call this faith, but I prefer to think of it as a simple awareness that we can't possibly know what is actually good or bad. It is only our idea of what we think 'should' happen that determines our sense of what we celebrate or condemn. I have seen enough to know that we haven't actually got a clue. Better instead to trust that all is as it should be. The Buddhists call this equanimity – seeing all things as equal.

....

THE SILVER LINING

When I first started running workshops, I used to do an exercise called 'Searching for the Silver Lining.' This involved giving people a series of seemingly 'bad' or difficult scenarios and asking them to be creative in coming up with 'good' outcomes, which would actually mean that these supposedly 'bad' situations were actually blessings in disguise. These started easily with a scenario of someone falling off a ladder and breaking an ankle. How could that be a good thing? That one is pretty simple. Maybe they would meet the future love of their life in the hospital. Or imagine that the broken ankle had prevented them from getting on a flight that went on to crash. Anything is possible. Sometimes the silver linings are easy to spot. At other times, it is not so easy.

The final hypothetical scenario from the workshop was getting people to try and find the potential silver lining from a story where their partner and children die in a fatal car accident caused by a drunk driver? Can you come up with a positive outcome that could, at some point in time, be OK or even see that as perfect? It took people much longer to do that but there are lots of possible silver linings for this outcome too, although I know you might have a hard time believing that right now.

It is difficult to remember at times that the silver lining might not be for your personal benefit. The silver lining might serve some wider benefit for the field of consciousness. Maybe you would go on to write the most amazing book on grieving that would soothe millions of other people who are suffering with losing a loved one? Maybe your neighbor would be so horrified at your loss that they would forevermore cherish their children in such a way that those children go on to have a completely different life? Maybe the motorist who killed your family may never ever drink again and become the best addiction worker the world has ever seen. Maybe you will lose your way so profoundly that someone else changes their life completely by discovering their greatest gifts in the saving of you?

....

I don't believe that we are here for us, and our idea of what is supposed to happen can prevent us from experiencing love at continuous sight. This is not some empty placation based on the idea that 'God moves in mysterious ways.' This instead is about demonstrating that it is our perspective and our attachment to things that prevent us from remaining at peace. The purpose of the silver lining exercise is to prove to you over and over again that it is possible to find a silver lining in every situation – to prove to yourself that it is all perspective. At that point, on some level, it is possible to stop looking for the silver lining and instead trust that it is there. Relax in the knowledge that everything is as it should be. This is about developing faith in the fact that you can look lovingly upon all things equally.

Please don't think that I underestimate the enormity of the grief of losing a beloved partner, parent, or child. I don't for a second. I hope my faith in the 'perfection' is never tested in that extreme way but I do know that if I lose my faith – if I am not able to see the value in the ugly ring or the lost loved one – I do know that when such things are weighed in my heart, it knows that all things are made of the same substance and therefore are all worth the same. Every person, every object, every moment, every heartbreak, every difficulty, and every situation are filled with the same pure golden light. Freedom is found in the ability to trust that. Destiny is found in having the wisdom to realize that, according to those same principles, there must be something golden and perfect about us.

Over the years I have been humbled by the extraordinary capacity the human heart has to find beautiful meaning and inspiring purpose in what was once the darkest of times. I have seen the deepest wounds be transformed into the most wonderful gifts. People often ask me if everything is perfect why are some people disabled? Why do some beautiful children get leukemia and only get to live until they are six?

From the personal perspective it can be very hard to see the perfection in some stories but very often the human spirit can be seen in its most exquisite beauty when a time calls for the greatest courage or the deepest love. If you speak to nurses who work in the hospices where some of these young children die, they will talk to you of humanity, kindness, compassion, and a true understanding of the value of every breath. If you look into the hearts of the parents who are losing a child you will see them cherish every single moment of that child. In the positive, upbeat, and playful spirit of that child there is a depth of courage that could inspire a nation.

At times we cannot possibly know why life is the way that it is, but every single moment is an opportunity to remember how blessed we are to be alive. Sometimes people are sacrificed for our remembrance. That is why making the most of life is so important. That is why it is vital that you, once and for all, drop the idea that there is anything wrong with you.

You are perfect and your purpose is about you falling in total love with yourself, creating a life that you adore and letting your light shine.

The greatest trick the ego ever played on our hearts was to convince our soul that its desire to shine was egotism. So many people on the spiritual path are driven to experience great and expanded ways of being, yet as they approach that possibility part of them pulls back because they fear what might happen. In truth, the ego is afraid of being dissolved and lost in the process. This is because at its core it knows that connecting spiritually involves a reconnection to the sense of oneness. In that field, the ego knows that its illusory separate and distinct nature will become clearer. It worries about its redundancy; it worries about becoming an irrelevance. It doesn't understand that the personality is a highly valuable operating system that enables our spirit to engage in the world. Through our personal essence we bring a unique flavor of spirit to the world through our personal preferences, desires, and passions.

If anything, spirituality enriches our personality because we are no longer so rigidly identified with it; we are less afraid and can have more fun with it. It frees us to SHINE as ourselves, in love with our identity and our divine role to play. Let yourself be an example of someone in love with themselves and life. Feeling connected, fulfilled, abundant, inspired, and deeply happy. This is your only real responsibility. This is your ultimate purpose. This brings unconditional love to life. This is the final YES of the FreeMind Experience. This brings absolute happiness to life.

FreeMind Purpose Practices

What follows are a number of different exercises and practices that you can start to experiment with, to help you connect more to the sense of oneness. These practices are about inspiring you to bring more of yourself to life: To love yourself and others unconditionally; to charge everything you do with a deep sense of joy and compassion, liveliness, and pleasure. When we are deeply connected to our universal and eternal nature we are more cheerful and playful. The FreeMind Experience is not about being more considered and contained. Our purpose is found most beautifully when we can enjoy the romance of each and every moment as we fall in love with absolutely everything.

At the end of this section there is also a list of recommended resources that can support you in becoming more purposeful (see page 237).

USING THE FREEMIND PRACTICES

When using the inner FreeMind Practices, it is important that you make yourself comfortable before you start – for example, ensure that you won't be disturbed, and allow plenty of time to do the process completely. When doing these exercises it is normal for your mind to wander and it is fine for you to move around to keep yourself comfortable. If possible:

* Do the exercises with your eyes comfortably closed.
* Allow yourself to become very still (your ability to do that will improve over time).
* Just take note of what you notice. You may find that some parts of the exercise are easier than others, but these are not things that you can get wrong.
* Don't get frustrated with yourself or think that these experiences have to be anything in particular.
* Keep an open mind. It is normal to have doubts.
* Give each exercise at least two good attempts. You may also notice that, at times, certain exercises won't work at all for you. In this case, try a different exercise or repeat it at a later time and you may respond differently.

As you allow yourself to go on these inner FreeMind journeys more and more, you may notice strange sensations, such as heaviness or lightness, in your body. You may even feel as if you are going numb. These are all perfectly normal reactions. You can stop whenever you want and your body will rapidly return to its usual sensations.

Wherever possible, become curious about the physical effects of the exercises. They are usually very positive signs that you have become deeply relaxed, which has been proven to be very good for both mind and body.

Some of the practices may take some getting used to but feel free to make them work for you. Be patient, generous, and collaborative. Don't hope they will 'do' something to you. Work with them to help them help you.

. . . .

FREEMIND PURPOSE PRACTICE 1

MEDITATION

The simplest way to reconnect to your sense of oneness is to take time out of your day to get fully relaxed and present. To do that, choose to sit for ten minutes and follow the instructions below. You can sit for longer if you want. This exercise is not about getting anywhere or achieving any kind of an experience. You may well be filled with a sense of connected bliss but that is more of a happy byproduct. Don't aim for that. Ideally this practice should be done while sitting upright with your back straight, your eyes closed, and your jaw relaxed. If you want to sit on a chair that is also fine. There are four simple steps to this process:

1. **Be totally still.** If you have to scratch or move your body that is fine, but return to stillness as soon as possible. Then stay totally still apart from your breathing, which ideally should be gentle and quiet, through the nose.
2. **Be at peace with 'what is.'** This doesn't mean that you should be totally peaceful or have a quiet mind. It doesn't matter what is happening in your mind and body. You simply notice what is happening and let everything be as

it is. Let the peacefulness have love in it for you and your experience.

3. **Pay attention.** This is about staying fully present to the moment-to-moment experience of being totally still (step 1) and being totally at peace (step 2). Instead of drifting off and not noticing your body, stay very aware of the feeling of your body being relaxed and still. This step is not passive. It is active. Feel into the experience.

4. **Hold a quarter-smile.** This would be barely visible on your face. It is the place your face goes to just before your smile breaks through. Try it now. Try a big smile. Then try a half-smile. Then a quarter-smile. Notice how internal it is. It creates an opening in the heart and an overall lift in the spirit. Adding this to your meditation (and your day) makes all of the difference.

You can do steps 1 to 4, and simply pay attention to being still and at peace, but you might also want to imagine breathing in blue sunshiny, positive, crisp, clean air, while breathing out old, tired, gray air. Imagining the whole time that your inner world is turning from dull and cloudy to bright and sunny. You might also want to spend time sending love and well wishes to your loved ones. You might want to include people you are upset with or people of whom you have been judgmental.

FREEMIND PURPOSE PRACTICE 2

DROPPING INTO THE VOID

For this visualization exercise, you might want to enlist the help of a friend who can talk you through the steps (or memorize the steps and take yourself through the process). See the resources section for music recommendations (page 237). Alternatively there is a beautiful version of this process set to powerfully evocative music in the FreeMind Home Training System (see page 238).

1. Use the meditation technique above or the relaxation techniques (see pages 167 or 169) to become very relaxed.

2. See yourself first in a beautiful summery meadow. Take some time to build up the sensory experience. Notice the colors and scents of the wild flowers, the sound of the grass underfoot, and the breeze in the trees.

3. Then notice that in the hillside ahead there is an opening to what looks to be a cave passageway. Pause before entering, knowing that something important is going to happen when you follow that path.

4. Enter and allow yourself to notice the temperature change. It is dark and the path is gently sloping down. It takes you a long way down, deep into the hillside. You can't see where you are going but know you must continue.

5. Then the passageway widens and you notice that the path has brought you out into a vast cavern that opens up above and below for what you sense are thousands of feet. The path goes out across the center and comes to an end. There is an endless drop on either side of the path. The vastness of the cavern is impossible to comprehend. Below there is a universe of emptiness. It is bottomless.

6. It remains dark but your eyes are adjusting and you notice that the path is now more like a thin plank of

stone reaching out over the abyss below. Walk to the end, turn around with your heels right on the edge of the plank. Raise both arms to your side. Feel the gravity calling you to fall off backward. This is an extreme trust game. A total surrender. A merging calling for your connection. A death waiting for your surrender.

7. Now let yourself simply fall off backwards. Keep breathing. You may panic at first, or feel quite dizzy. Fall into the deep dark blackness. Keep your breath calm and steady as you fall into what first feels like emptiness. Keep feeling into it, dissolving any resistance. Keep allowing yourself to surrender to the experience completely. Keep breathing deeply and opening to the experience.

8. Consciously choose to imagine the top of your head is opening. At the same time let yourself feel the area below your belly button opening. Focus on the feeling of a channel opening up through your whole center and out through every area of your body.

8. Keep breathing deeply and calmly, and allow the feeling of opening in your body to create a change in the darkness. Notice a chink of light, an opening. Feel and see the dark empty nothingness as it is transformed into a light-filled, connected everythingness. Dissolve into the experience. Go from disconnection and death to reconnection and eternity. Dissolve and arrive at the same time.

9. Become totally still; breathe light and life through every part of your extended being. Feel yourself as the whole universe. The forests, the deserts, the oceans, all of the planets and the stars, and identify most with all of that glorious space in between.

10. Listen to deeply honoring and celebratory music, and love yourself and life in its entirety.

FREEMIND PURPOSE PRACTICE 3

DEATHBED QUESTIONNAIRE

Imagine yourself on your deathbed right now and cast your mind back across your life. What would stand out? What memories would surface as the golden moments? Take a moment to consider this ...

Would it be vacations? If so, then that might suggest that your life is not fully a reflection of your greatest potential. This is not true in every case but these following questions are always worth checking in with every year, or certainly at every funeral.

* Are you living fully?
* Do you love fully?
* Are you happy?
* If you were given one more hour to live, how would you feel about your life?

As discussed (see page 211) it is a truly wise person who plans their deathbed experience. Plan to be at peace on your deathbed by making the most of this precious life now. Make a to-do list, prioritize it, and even set dates to do things by. Take it step by step and make the necessary changes to ensure that you are living and loving your life to the full.

FREEMIND PURPOSE PRACTICE 4

ANONYMOUS LOVE LETTER

This exercise involves writing a love letter to someone you don't know. This is an unconditional expression of love that you then place in an envelope and leave for some random stranger to find. This is not about sending a love letter to someone you know. It is a message of love given unconditionally, which is based on the idea that everyone is deserving of love and we are capable of loving everyone. It is a good practice and can be an incredibly beautiful experience. This is anonymous, so don't sign your name or leave contact details on there.

Although it can be fun to leave the letter on the seat next to you on the bus and then stay to see who picks it up, I wouldn't recommend doing do that. The exercise is about you enjoying sending out love and letting it go. It is not about getting a 'kick' out of seeing who gets it and the effect it creates.

It's also amazing to do this exercise with a group of friends but, before you take the letters out onto the streets, mix the letters up and all randomly take one to read. When you experience how beautiful receiving these letters can be, you will get excited to write more. You might also want to encourage the recipient, if they have enjoyed the letter, to then go on to write their own for someone else to find. If you feel so inclined, and only if it feels good, you could explain in your letter that you got the idea from reading this book.

Another nice touch is to write 'For you' on the front of the envelope, and then 'Yes you' on the back.

If you're wondering what you might write, what would

you write to your child (or a child that you love) to help them feel willing to open their heart to the world and inspire them to make the most of their life? Or consider what piece of wisdom you would most like to be reminded of? Share that today. That message could save someone's life.

I cannot recommend this exercise enough. I took a team of people to a number of festivals and ended up getting thousands of people to write love letters, which we then sent out through the festival as viral messages of love. (The letters were designed to be read and then passed on.) The reports back from people who had received the perfect message at the perfect moment were amazing.

FREEMIND PURPOSE PRACTICE 5

LOVE SONG PLAYLIST

Create a playlist of your favorite love songs and choose to listen to them as a love song from you to you, or you could listen to it as a love song from your heart to your mind, from your future great self to your present-day self. You could imagine the song is from the universe to you, from God to you, or from Mother Earth to you. This sounds simple, but if you choose the right song, the effect can be incredible. Check out some of the recommended music at the end of this section if you need some inspiration (see page 237).

FREEMIND PURPOSE PRACTICE 6

BLESS YOUR DAY

According to the principles of Oneness Philosophy, all things and all people are an absolute expression of the divine. On that basis, everyone you meet is a representative of the divine. You are the outstretched hand of the divine in the perfect place at the perfect time, and so is everyone else.

Set aside a day to consciously choose to see everyone and everything as the divine. Spend a day practicing the art of love at continuous sight. Meet your moment unconditionally. Hear every word as an expression of the divine. Feel every touch as an expression of the divine. You can work up to a full day if that feels easier by starting with an hour at a time. Notice how amazing you feel when you consciously set out to be a fully loving and accepting being.

Remember to include loving and honoring your boundaries on this day. Loving your day completely also includes loving that part of you that wants to say 'NO' to something that someone asks of you. Unconditional love is not about becoming a walkover and saying 'YES' to every request or letting people do whatever they want. Always love in ways that honor your precious boundaries.

FREEMIND PURPOSE PRACTICE 7

BLESS YOUR EXPERIENCE

Before you do anything, you can choose to ritualize it as a divine experience. This is hugely about the power of intention and expectation. This exercise is one of the best ways to bring your spirit to life. For example, you might choose to:

* Bless your bath as a ritual designed to wash away your fear and soothe your soul.
* Take a moment before you eat to bless the food and feel gratitude for everything that has brought it to your table.
* Bless water with healing or holy qualities before you drink it. You have as much authority as anyone else to do this (I promise).
* Listen to music with the sole purpose of connecting to the divine.
* Go for a massage and choose to experience it as the hands of the divine giving you the massage.

Use the following steps as a guideline. Once you become practiced at blessing things, you'll be able to do it in a matter of seconds. It is also fine to spend a long time over this exercise if you want to do it very deeply. Feel free to create your own version of this. Most important, have fun with it.

1. Close your eyes and take a moment to get fully present in your body.
2. Deepen your breathing and feel yourself opening your heart.
3. Allow peace and love to spread through you.
4. Take a moment to appreciate yourself and life.
5. Tell yourself that what you are about to experience is an opportunity for you to:
   * Connect to yourself.
   * Feel loved.

* Feel inspired.
* Be reminded of what you need to be reminded of.
* Be connected to nature/Mother Earth/God.
* Be healed.
* Or possibly all of the above.

6. Then see yourself briefly enjoying the experience and being filled and flooded with the result or benefit that you are welcoming in as a blessing.

7. If you are blessing something physical (for example, food or a bath), you might also want to hold your hands over the object, and feel as though you are pouring love and power into this object. Imagine that your hands have the power to transmit or connect this object to all of this positive energy. Feel it happening.

8. Say a vision statement (see page 171) as a final blessing.

9. Then enjoy the experience with as much presence and concentration as possible. Savor it as an absolute meditation. Feel yourself being nourished, fulfilled, inspired, and so on. Feel it as a direct opportunity to connect with the loving, all-powerful universe.

FREEMIND PURPOSE PRACTICE 8

THE POWER OF NATURE

The best way to connect to your grander sense of self is to stay connected to nature. Get out into nature as much as possible and, if possible, get your bare feet on the ground and your hands dirty. A few other ideas might be:

* Celebrate the changing seasons in your home.

* Make sure you have plants and, ideally, some kind of running water in or near your home.
* Pay attention to the phases of the moon.
* Visit the ocean as much as you can.

Being in a natural environment, it is easier to remember that you ARE nature. This makes living in balance so much easier.

FREEMIND PURPOSE PRACTICE 9

BOOMERANG LETTER

This exercise involves writing a letter from one part of you and then writing another letter as a response from another part of you. Writing these letters can be absolutely fascinating, and give you a deep understanding of why things are happening. It can also give you insight into how best to approach things moving forward.

You might choose to address this letter to your heart, to your inner mind, to the universe or, if it suits your beliefs, to God. You can also use this technique to speak to a part of you that is responsible for a certain behavior that you would like to change.

When you write the letter back, it can feel a little contrived in the beginning because you know it is you writing the letter. However, after a few moments you might be surprised to notice that it really does feel that what is being written is coming 'through' you as opposed to 'from you.'

According to the principles of Oneness Philosophy, you are everything and everybody so you can send and receive a letter to and from anything in the universe. For example, you could write a letter to the Sun, and no doubt you will get a beautiful response.

The intelligence that runs this world is you, and your unconscious mind wants to communicate with you to help you live with more love and freedom. It has a huge amount to say about how you are living and what you could be doing differently. Use this exercise to simply open up the channel.

1. You will need two different colored pens and plenty of blank paper.

2. Start with a big rant and let all your negative emotions, frustrations, and complaints about yourself and life pour out of you. Keep the pen moving and don't think about what you are writing. Don't stop for at least five minutes, even if your writing becomes gibberish, keep the pen moving. Include questions and confusions. Ask for answers, insights, and instructions about doing or seeing things differently.

3. When you are finished, take a moment to close your eyes, breathe deeply, and let all of those feelings settle down a bit.

4. Now imagine reading the letter as if you were the respondent, and imagine you know exactly what to say. Trust that it will come through.

5. Now, pick up the other pen and let the response come back. Again, this may feel a little contrived at first but once you get into the swing of it, you may be surprised how much wisdom and understanding you are connected to.

6. If appropriate, make agreements with yourself. Prioritize

your actions. Set dates on the agreements and take action immediately. Let the first step be small, so that it is easy, then do it.

RECOMMENDED RESOURCES

MUSIC

* Florence & the Machine, *Never Let Me Go*: An exquisite song about finally relaxing into oneness. Possibly the most perfect lyrics ever.
* John Barry, *The Beyondness of Things*: A sumptuous modern classical piece filled with a feeling of gratitude and joy.
* Jont, *Supernatural*: An amazing song about the part of us that wants to merge with oneness; and the interplay between the part of us which is scared to connect that deeply.
* Jont, *The Way Home*: A beautiful song with amazing lyrics about coming back to the center; coming back to the home of the heart.
* Sebastien Tellier, *La Ritournelle*: An evocative and celebratory piece of motivational dance music that invites you to fall in love with yourself and life – beautiful.

BOOKS

* Greg Braden, *The Divine Matrix*: An incredible look at the world of subatomic physics, oneness, and the conscious universe.
* Nisargadatta Maharaj, *I Am That*: An advanced and

complicated, but brilliant look at oneness, the mind, and the possibilities of freedom.

* Ramana Maharshi, *Be As You Are*: A beautiful encouragement to rest in your natural perfection.

FREEMIND RESOURCES

* **The Benefits of a Free Mind** A short video explaining the simple logic of the benefits of living with more love and peace in your life. For more information, visit www. freemindproject.org/reprogramming or scan the QR code below.

* **FreeMind Home Training System** This enables you to connect deeply with your sense of oneness. The training recordings combine all of the FreeMind Principles and Practices, with powerful hypnosis and metaphorically charged bespoke film score music. This home training system also includes short support and inspirational videos. For more information, see Further FreeMind Resources, page 253, visit www.freemindproject. org/3pillars or scan the QR code below.

The Seeds Coming into Bloom

Peace, Power, and Purpose are the Three Pillars of absolute happiness. When we have deprogrammed all of the limiting ideas, feelings, and beliefs, we can experience great levels of Peace – Pillar 1. When we reprogram ourselves with empowered beliefs and inspiring feelings we can unleash our ultimate Power – Pillar 2. When we Reconnect our experience of ourselves as the great and universal whole, we can love all things equally and we see all things as being perfect – Pillar 3. Pillar 1 means we are able to say 'YES' to everything that has ever happened to us. Pillar 2 means we are able to say 'YES' to ourselves completely. Pillar 3 means we are able to say 'YES' to the whole of life in each and every divine moment.

That Triple YES means you will be fully present in each moment, knowing that it is an invitation for you to simply be a joyful living expression of your ultimate peace and power. Your purpose then is to find the courage to truly be yourself and to create the life that you deeply love.

THREE PILLARS BECOME ONE

While there are discrete principles and practices in each pillar, as you develop each of these areas of your life, the Three Pillars soon become totally interlinked. The more you connect to the sense of oneness, the more peaceful and powerful you will feel. The more you unleash your power, the more peaceful and connected you will feel. The more you enjoy feeling peaceful, the more powerful and connected you will be. Therefore the work that you do in each area underpins the development of each other area too. It all works cumulatively. In your ultimate moments of enlightenment your peace, power, and purpose all become one.

THERE IS NO ENLIGHTENED END POINT

Many people start out on the spiritual path hoping to gain something from it. Very soon their practice is driven by the idea that there is 'somewhere' to go and 'something' to get. This very often focuses around a fantasy of total enlightenment: The idea that there is a place that we 'get to' where all of our troubles melt away, a place where we are ultimately free forever. The FreeMind Experience is not about arriving at some end point. It is about integrating principles and practices into your life, so that you can have a different relationship with those parts of yourself that are scared, resistant, competitive, and essentially unhappy.

There is no place to get to where you will be free of your fear. But, with practice, you can change how that fear impacts you. With awareness, you can continually bring yourself back to a perspective that brings more peace, power and purpose to your life. However, it is really important that you don't think of that peace, power, and purpose as something that needs to be added to you. The FreeMind Practices are simply about bringing your attention to who you really are, already in this moment. They help you to experience your natural perfection, right now. Your hand was once the hand of a baby. A perfect little being who couldn't do anything wrong. No expectations, no failings, nothing needing to be different. Take a moment to look at your hand now and see the perfection of you in this moment. Be a loving deity to yourself. Open your heart to yourself as you would (or have) to your own child.

RE-PARENTING

The FreeMind Experience is, in many ways, about you re-parenting yourself. Giving yourself the perfect love and support that you need as you develop, so that you can find your way in the world with effectiveness, happiness, and joy. Yes, this is about healing old wounds from your past, but also about relating to yourself in that way now. Being there for yourself as a constant loving guiding light. Your unconscious (or soul) is ever ready to guide you toward your full self-expression.

My mother says, 'You love your children, but you are IN love with your grandchildren.' In many ways, the love a grandparent feels for their grandchildren is unconditional. Our own kids are a reflection of us. How they behave therefore means something about us as parents. But for the grandparents, that extra layer of generational distance means they can just love their grandkids to bits — it is truly unconditional. So, if you are struggling to develop a loving relationship with yourself by thinking of being your own parent, think instead of being a loving grandparent to yourself.

SELF-AWARENESS

The process of becoming more self-aware can be incredibly challenging. Unearthing our limiting beliefs, resolving our resentments, making amends, and trying to live with integrity, accountability, and honor can take some doing. It is essential therefore that you are gentle with yourself along the way. Part of that is managing your expectations and knowing that there are going to be some struggles, there are going to be some challenges. Try your best to see these as opportunities to develop your self. See life in those difficult moments as a character gym: A chance for you to become more peaceful and powerful. All your difficulties are an invitation to find more freedom. All the conflict, confusion, and pain in your life are calling you to look at unresolved thoughts, feelings, beliefs, and behaviors. All of your negative emotions are coming from a part of you that would really benefit from more loving support and understanding.

THE PERFECTION IN THE FALL

It is important to remember that we can't step out of the realm of perfection. Our connection is never really lost and, no matter how far we feel we have strayed from our true and happy path, our perfection is there every step of the way to love and support us. We are either moving toward our loving and peaceful self or we are moving toward our fearful and unhappy self. However, both are perfect.

If you drop the idea of 'good' and 'bad' and instead look at the labels of 'efficient' and 'educational,' it is easier to see the perfection in all things. If we are in flow and everything is aligned, things work well and easily. We could call that 'efficient.' If, in contrast, we are identifying with our limited and fearful self – we are contracted and difficult, defensive, competitive, and so on – then things are less likely to work. On that path we are likely to experience friction. To begin with, we may experience dissatisfaction or mild anxiety but if it continues we may feel heavily depressed and deeply unhappy. If things remain out of balance, then we may be brought down to our knees by some awful illness, have an accident, or be attacked.

These dark feelings and difficult situations are not punishments. They are not evidence of you being outside of the love of the universe. They are love in reverse. Take the courage to feel into these difficult feelings, and you'll find that they are packed full of information and inspiration to help you find your way back into alignment with your amazing, loving, and positive self. They are not reprimands. They are signposts. In every one of your most difficult moments, you were being rebalanced. This was an invitation for you to find your way back home. So, on that basis, it is possible to realize that you no longer have good and bad days. You could instead imagine that you are having either efficient or educational days: fantastic (lots of gratitude) days or fascinating (lots of learning) days. We are either in alignment and blessed or we are being shown what is taking us out of alignment. Both are love in action.

In your darkest moments love is trying to bring you home.

Any time you find yourself at a crossroads and don't know which way to go, take heart in realizing that there is no wrong path. To my reckoning, every day brings at least three important opportunities to bring my heart to life. When you find yourself in those situations today, I invite you to simply ask yourself the following question. The answer always gives the best guidance on which way to go. It is the ultimate compass for absolute happiness.

What is the truth and what would love do?

(The answer to this question must include what love would do for you too.)

SUMMARY: THE FREEMIND THREE PILLARS

Here below is a recap of the Three Pillars. I have also included the internal effect and the external effect of each pillar. The internal effect is what you will feel as you integrate the principles and practices of each pillar into your life. The external effect is what other people will see and experience when dealing with you once you have integrated the principles and practices of the Three Pillars into your life.

FREEMIND EXPERIENCE

	Pillar 1: Peace	Pillar 2: Power	Pillar 3: Purpose
Process	Deprogramming	Reprogramming	Reconnection
Practice	Emotional Intelligence	Success Psychology	Oneness Philosophy
Internal effect	Grace and gratitude	Flow and fulfillment	Connection and love
External effect	Compassionate and calm	Confident and charismatic	Passionate and playful
Dark side	Spiritual bypass	Spiritual materialism	Spiritual activism

COMMUNITY IS A VITAL PART OF LIVING A FREE AND HAPPY LIFE

As you become more conscious, it is likely that you'll want to connect with other conscious people. Going out, getting drunk, and having shallow and repetitive conversations will lose their appeal. What we crave is an authentic community where we are inspired by each other to be our very best. To meet others in ways where it is natural for us to be open, honest, and undefended. This is why so many people get addicted to going on workshops because they get to be truly themselves. These training environments can be challenging but most people come away from them feeling seen, appreciated, inspired, and, most of all, connected. It is in these places that we can experience a real sense of being at home. This sensation is the experience of what it is like to be in a real community.

When we get a taste of it, we crave it. When we were hunter-gatherers, we were part of large clans. It wasn't like the current model of the two-parent satellite family wandering the Earth with 2.4 children. Anthropologists say that it is much more likely that we roamed in groups of about 12 but were part of a bigger clan (community) of between 50 and 100. There is strength in numbers and also beauty. In community we can't really get away with being inauthentic. It simply won't work. A healthy community unintentionally holds up a mirror to us, inviting us to operate with greater levels of integrity and capability. In community, we are stretched and appreciated, inspired and driven to be our best for each other and ourselves. When we are in community, our place in the world is confirmed, our core values are refreshed, and so our understanding of what is actually important in life is kept close to heart and mind.

In indigenous communities they maintain their cultural health and identity by using rituals, rites of passage, and sacred celebrations. In many areas of modern life we have lost these vital aspects. That is why I am now passionate about creating transformational experiences and events that use ritual and rites of passage to help people relate to themselves in more empowered ways. Getting people out of workshops and getting their feet on the earth, getting them round a fire, using music, dancing, and, at times, terrifying challenges (rites of passage) are all incredibly powerful ways of inspiring us to be our very best. Dry, theoretical training events are not the way forward. I believe that personal development should be a wide-eyed, wild ride of pleasure and passion. Bringing out your best should be a blast!

THE IMPORTANCE OF CONSCIOUS CELEBRATION

The final and, I believe, most essential part of living a free and happy life is conscious celebration. So many people are addicted to working on themselves, looking at what isn't working and fixing it. There is, of course, a place for that, but it is also hugely important for us to come together to simply celebrate the absolute joy of life. Building friendships and communities that come together regularly to remind us of the meaning of life is vital. Remembering the joy to be found in you being your most peaceful, playful, and passionate self is an essential part of living and loving life to the full. Otherwise your spiritual practice runs the risk of making you really boring. Becoming conscious is about becoming more alive. It is not about becoming more considered and contained.

Partying, laughing, dancing, singing, and appreciating beautiful live music and talented performers are the best reminders that life is wonderful. Life is so short, so it is important to put regular plans in place to fill your life with the things that make it joyful. In the Further FreeMind

Resources section (see page 253), you can find out more about the FreeMind Celebrations that we run and the celebration templates and guidelines we give away, so that you can start building your own positive and loving communities that will support and inspire you to live and love life to the full.

....

THE ABSOLUTE HAPPINESS OF PEACE, POWER, AND PURPOSE

When I was very little, I used to have a recurring dream. I would be looking down on what looked like an animation of a rapidly moving ball of string. Like a live ball of wriggling spaghetti that would be frantically moving all around. In the dream, I would descend into the ball of string and all of its energy would fill and surround me. I would be the frenetic chaos of everything, jumbled, stressed, constantly moving, and turning. It made me feel slightly nauseous. Not to the point of feeling sickly, more a feeling of 'movement overwhelm' – vertiginous on entering and immediately exhausting. Not only were all the thousand threads moving rapidly, breathing in and out, but they were also vibrating at incredibly high frequencies.

It felt and sounded like being surrounded by a million bees, but then something would change. One thread would stand out. Its vibration would be so powerful that I would be drawn to it. As I focused on it, the intensity of its vibration would amplify, the strand would widen. If you have ever twanged the low string on a guitar, or even better a double bass, you would get a sense of what I was looking at – an intense quivering back and forth of pure vibration from which emanated the deepest of tones. In the dream, the tone became utterly compelling. There was something vastly addictive about it. The dream would change into a chase for that vibration.

Somehow, I would find myself seeking that feeling and all the strings around me would intensify, every part of me was jagged and bubbling with a million different vibrations all doing different things and then, suddenly, I would find that one string and its vibration would open up and I would fall into total harmony with it, and then there would be nothing. All the strings had become one string. All the variation of vibrations had become one encompassing vibration of everything. All the hectic-ness disappeared. My whole body sang out with one vibration filled with all vibrations. My eyes would roll into the back of my head as bliss flooded my whole system. I was gone.

But then, a staccato drum, a snap, a stutter, a splutter and, like falling out of a moving car, I would fall out of harmony and all of the jumbled-ness would reappear. I would be in the hectic ball of string, bounced around like in the most ferocious bubbly Jacuzzi. The dream would continue like this for ages. An ongoing interplay of being in and then out, of being disconnected and connected. I can still remember the feeling of release and freedom associated with those moments of interconnected bliss.

....

INNER FREEDOM

In the middle of a fast-spinning wheel, there is a center point that is still. There is a place of freedom inside all of us where, no matter what is happening on the outside, we have the capacity to stay centered, calm, loving, and peaceful. All of us have the ability to live totally in truth and, therefore, to charge everything we do with immense power. When we have the courage to truly be ourselves, we vibrate with energy of an intense clarity that makes others stop and listen; people believe in us, people want to help us, and people want us to help them. When we can operate from that beautiful place of peace and power, everything we do flows with a kind of blessed grace that is specific to us. We move with a signature tone that automatically lines things up around us. We attract the right people and we repel those that are not aligned with who we are, or what we are being led to do.

With this level of alignment and congruent embodiment, we have a line of insight and understanding that reaches way beyond our normal intelligence. In those moments, we can shine with brilliance because we are connected to everything that has ever been known. That doesn't mean we always know what to do but we do know that we are in the right place at the right time with everything we need, to do whatever needs to be done.

Our freedom, then, isn't dependent on us being brilliant but rather the certainty that in life's uncertainty there is safety. We remain clear and calm, when others panic; we have the resilience and the resolution to weather the harshest of difficulties. We see all suffering as an opportunity for growth and compassion. We see our conditioning as the last remnants of old ideas that no longer serve us and we allow them, bit by bit, to dissolve away. Because we can look upon our darkness with love, we breathe light into our lives and compassion into the lives of others. As we hold out our darkness, cupped in hands of love, our infancy is warmed through and our fears are integrated into a whole, where they are transformed into endless insight and understanding.

We finally become adult, whole, and complete. Our place is not seen as a final destination but more of a collaboration of tones: A bringing together of a symphony of vibrations, a whirling mass of perfection waiting to be unified by the purest love warming the heart of your being. Where, as one voice, one singular song, one vibration of all tones, we are ultimately aligned with all of the creative forces of the universe. Where we are the one song. We are the *uni-verse* in all of its glory.

RETURNING HOME TO UNCONDITIONAL LOVE

The remembrance of our true nature beyond our conditioned sense of separation is our holy journey. Our language patterns, our limited vocabulary, our socialized conditioning, the tyranny of the ego's confusion, the darkness of the world of advertising, the messaging on individuality, the forgetting of our connection to the natural world, the pollution of our minds and bodies, the destructiveness of the modern working environment, the loss of community and the built-up wounds of inter-generational familial suffering all prevent us from remembering our natural, positive, and loving blissful state. What then can be done to find that tune again? How can we hum it back to each other? Where is middle 'C'? What can be done about it? Not because it should be, but instead, because it can be. How can we find joy in the process of our awareness re-experiencing the connection that was never actually severed?

The answer again returns to the eternal theme of unconditional love. Only the interplay of falling in and out of love explains this everlasting game. That is the invite. That is the exploration. The journey back to love is not a chore to be endured. It is a romance to be enjoyed. It is the courtship of our highest potential. It is the coy smile of possibility spreading through our being gathering belief as it expands. It is love rediscovering itself time and time again. Yes you, yes now. Yes you and yes now, exactly as you are – on and off in your awareness for eternity.

* Nothing is wrong.
* Nothing needs to be done.
* No one is in control.
* No one is responsible.
* Don't take anything personally.
* Let forgiveness evolve into gratitude.
* Follow your desires.
* Honor your boundaries.
* Find joy in what you do.
* Live in truth.
* Live with love.
* Let your light shine.

Tom Fortes Mayer, May 23, 2014

Further FreeMind Resources

FREEMIND HOME TRAINING SYSTEM

Take the life-changing principles and practices of FreeMind, combine them with advanced hypnosis and specially designed soundscapes, and you have the perfect recipe for bringing more love and happiness to your life. Imagine having the very best tools and techniques at the tips of your fingers whenever you need them most. With that guidance, healing, and inspiration on tap you can overcome your difficulties, unleash your potential, and connect more deeply to yourself and others. With over ten years of extensive design and development this system is at the cutting edge of life-change technology.

The system includes:

* Motivational training on the transformational principles and practices of FreeMind.

* Fully guided hypnosis journeys designed to heal, inspire, and empower.
* Short motivational recordings to keep your energy and inspiration high during the day.
* A whole range of different guided meditations and contemplations that create life change.
* Hundreds of tips and techniques for bringing more peace, power, and purpose to your life.
* Specially designed music that powerfully evokes emotions and drives unconscious change.
* A series of inspirational, supporting, and instructional videos by Tom Fortes Mayer.
* Step-by-step instructions on how best to use FreeMind to get the best result.

The benefits you will experience:

* Dissolving of old patterns, behaviors, and feelings that hold you back.
* Having more confidence in yourself and enthusiasm for life.
* More purpose, passion, and joy in your life.
* More resilience, dynamism, life balance, health, and energy.
* More beautiful and successful relationships at home, at work, and with friends and family.
* Enjoying more happiness, success, and abundance in your life.

*With today's technology people
can safely do the deepest work
on themselves in the comfort of
their own home for a fraction of the
cost and disruption associated with
traditional therapy.*
Tom Fortes Mayer

For more information on this training and to see testimonial videos visit www.freemindproject.org/3pillars or scan the QR code below.

FREEMIND TRAINING

Improving your life is something to be celebrated. Coming together with other people to go on a wild and wide-eyed journey of self-discovery and self-improvement is a grand opportunity for a powerful rite of passage. All FreeMind Training events are immersive, celebratory learning environments that lovingly pull you into new and exciting ways of being more in keeping with your natural essence. This is not about fixing you. This is about allowing any old and limiting ideas simply to be dissolved away in an absolute furnace of love, appreciation, and inspiration.

Imagine going away to a place of great natural beauty and being surrounded by many other incredible people, all on a journey to become fully expressed loving people making the very most of this precious life. Imagine exquisite live music, delicious healthy food, loving facilitation, deep insights, provocative training, beautiful artistic performances, inspirational stories, powerful challenges, playful interactions, late-night fires, and sacred sunrises all designed to help you love yourself and your life more.

* Step away from any old patterns or limiting identities.
* Unleash and embody your greatest shining potential.
* Deeply integrate the FreeMind Principles and Practices into your life.
* Become part of a loving and supportive community.
* Be immersed in a world of health, harmony, and happiness.
* Be inspired to live and love your life to the full.

Personal development is the new rock 'n' roll.
Tom Fortes Mayer

Come and inspire your mind, warm your heart, cherish your body, and nourish your soul. For more information go to: www.freemindproject.org/training or scan the QR code below.

FREEMIND CELEBRATIONS

A vital part of living and loving life to the full is celebration. It is important that we come together with the people we love to remind ourselves of what is truly amazing and beautiful about life.

Go to www.freemindproject.org/celebrations to get information on the up and coming FreeMind celebrations or scan the QR code below.

Alternatively, use the following guidelines to create your own FreeMind conscious party.

* Bring lots of lovely people together, young and old.
* As a group bless the experience with a positive intention (see page 232).
* Give people a chance to create, collaborate, and contribute to make it happen.
* Bring lots of lovely things to enjoy (that is, music, food, games, movies, songs, stories, jokes).
* Be lovely and loving with each other on purpose.
* Encourage people to express themselves and perform. (All standards welcome.)
* Create personal intentions/resolutions and express them to each other.

* Dance your dreams to life. Literally embody your most free and happy self. (Go to the FreeMind website for recommended music and pre-mixed dance sets.)
* Hug a lot, give massages, foot rubs, head rubs, hair stroking, and so on.
* Eat food together.
* Repeat regularly.

Parties are the most beautiful way to bring your best to life.
Tom Fortes Mayer

FREEMIND PROJECT (REGISTERED CHARITY NO. 1126454)

FreeMind donates 50 percent of its profits to the FreeMind Project charity, which is dedicated to researching, planning, implementing, and promoting more loving and enlightened ways of living.

We do this by:

* Training, developing, supporting, and promoting other positive change-makers and good causes that we believe in.
* Creating training and inspirational films for the dissemination and promotion of more wise and loving ways to live.

* Promoting the FreeMind Three Pillars in the fields of parenting, education, employment, healthcare, mental health, addiction treatment, prison rehabilitation, youth engagement, community building, economics, and government.
* When the Three Pillars of Emotional Intelligence, Success Psychology, and Oneness Philosophy factor much more highly in society's value system, our world will naturally become a much more beautiful place.
* We are not pushing from despair, we are flowing peacefully from the great belief we have in the human heart.
* This is a logical loving revolution.
* This is simply about bringing more love and peace to life.

By buying FreeMind products, coming to FreeMind events or watching the free FreeMind films you are helping us make the world a more beautiful place.

To get involved or for more information go to www. freemindproject.org/charity or scan the QR code below.

Endnotes

1. *The Great Sperm Race*, Blink Films & Cream Productions (first aired Channel 4, UK, June 21, 2009).
2. All is forgiven Paul, wherever you are.
3. I was committed to helping companies create inspirational working environments and so encourage the next generation of employees to engage with work and life in more meaningful, positive, and productive ways.
4. It is unfortunate that in today's world some of these case studies could be held against my clients, for example, when applying for a job or trying to adopt. There is still so much fear that surrounds emotional difficulties and mental health that such disclosures put them in danger of being negatively affected. I have therefore decided to obscure their identities to protect them. However, as you read their stories, please be aware that nearly all of them were willing to share their truth without the need of anonymity or defense. They and I feel that there is absolutely no shame in having emotional challenges or existential conflict. I believe that is the 'normal' state of affairs for most people. The more honest and open we can be about that, the better things will get for

everyone. It is not our madness that causes trouble. It is our resistance to it, our fear of it, and the shame that surrounds it. Once we are free, we can usually see the perfection in the pattern, and the telling of the story reveals that beauty. In honor of that I share these stories with you now.

5. Rosenthal, R. and Jacobson, L., 'Pygmalion in the Classroom,' *The Urban Review*, September 1968; 3(1): 16–20; http://link.springer.com/article/10.1007/BF02322211#page-1

6. Randomly taking messages from books is a school of divination or fortune-telling called bibliomancy.

7. *Fear and Faith*, Derren Brown, produced by Derren Brown for Channel 4, UK (first aired Channel 4, November 2012).

8. This doesn't mean that you got the job, passed the exam, seduced the perfect partner, or delivered the best presentation. It just means that you did your best. Maybe, in fact, you didn't do that well, but you did better than last time. Maybe you did worse than last time but you sincerely tried to do well. Any of these would still mean you deserve to be proud of how you are operating.

9. Gisin, N., 'Entanglement for Enhanced Encryption Security and Quantum Computers,' Geneva University, Development in Photon; www.geneva.ch/entanglement.htm.

10. Libet, B. *et al.*, 'Time of Conscious Intention to Act in Relation to Onset of Cerebral Activity (Readiness-Potential – The Unconscious Initiation of a Freely Voluntary Act,' *Brain*, 1983; 106: 623–42. doi: 10.1093/brain-106.3.623.

WATKINS

Sharing Wisdom Since
1893

The story of Watkins Publishing dates back to March 1893, when John M. Watkins, a scholar of esotericism, overheard his friend and teacher Madame Blavatsky lamenting the fact that there was nowhere in London to buy books on mysticism, occultism or metaphysics. At that moment Watkins was born, soon to become the home of many of the leading lights of spiritual literature, including Carl Jung, Rudolf Steiner, Alice Bailey and Chögyam Trungpa.

Today our passion for vigorous questioning is still resolute. With over 350 titles on our list, Watkins Publishing reflects the development of spiritual thinking and new science over the past 120 years. We remain at the cutting edge, committed to publishing books that change lives.

DISCOVER MORE ...

Read our blog   Watch and listen to   Sign up to
our authors in action   our mailing list

JOIN IN THE CONVERSATION

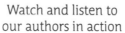

f WatkinsPublishing   **y** @watkinswisdom

▶ WatkinsPublishingLtd   **8+** +watkinspublishing1893

Our books celebrate conscious, passionate, wise and happy living.
Be part of the community by visiting

www.watkinspublishing.com